# The Laughter of Sarah

DOI: 10.1057/9781137370914

*Also by Catherine Conybeare*

*Paulinus Noster: Self and Symbols in the Letters of Paulinus of Nola* (2000)
*The Irrational Augustine* (2006)

DOI: 10.1057/9781137370914

palgrave▶**pivot**

▶

# The Laughter of Sarah:
# Biblical Exegesis,
# Feminist Theory, and the
# Concept of Delight

Catherine Conybeare

# palgrave
# macmillan

DOI: 10.1057/9781137370914

THE LAUGHTER OF SARAH
Copyright © Catherine Conybeare, 2013.

First published in 2013 by
PALGRAVE MACMILLAN®
in the United States—a division of St. Martin's Press LLC,
175 Fifth Avenue, New York, NY 10010.

Where this book is distributed in the UK, Europe and the rest of the world,
this is by Palgrave Macmillan, a division of Macmillan Publishers Limited,
registered in England, company number 785998, of Houndmills,
Basingstoke, Hampshire RG21 6XS.

Palgrave Macmillan is the global academic imprint of the above companies
and has companies and representatives throughout the world.

Palgrave® and Macmillan® are registered trademarks in the United States, the
United Kingdom, Europe and other countries.

ISBN: 978–1–137–37098–3  EPUB
ISBN: 978–1–137–37091–4  PDF
ISBN: 978–1–137–37311–3   Hardback

Library of Congress Cataloging-in-Publication Data is available from
the Library of Congress.

A catalogue record of the book is available from the British Library.

First edition: 2013

www.palgrave.com/pivot

DOI: 10.1057/9781137370914

*For Hilary*

DOI: 10.1057/9781137370914

DOI: 10.1057/9781137370914

Published by Novello & Company Limited
Printed in Great Britain by The Novello Press Limited, Sevenoaks, Kent

I Would Be True.
Words by Howard Walter.
Music by Herbert Howells.

DOI: 10.1057/9781137370914

# Contents

DOI: 10.1057/9781137370914

# Prelude

More than thirty years ago now, as children in Oxford, my sister and I received an invitation to tea. Two little girls of our own age had come down from London to visit their grandparents: we were supposed to go and keep them company.

The four of us barely knew each other, and conversation soon faltered. There was nothing to do and an eternity before our parents would come to collect us. Then one of the visitors remembered a game.

The game was very simple. We all knelt on the floor in a rather square circle. We bowed into the center of the circle, intoning in chorus, "Sad and solemn occasion." Then the leader fixed me in the eye and said with a sigh, "Catherine, this is a sad and solemn occasion." We all bowed and intoned; and then I had to respond, while gazing at her with equal intensity, "Yes, Emma, this is indeed a sad and solemn occasion." We bowed again, and it was my turn to select one of the others and advise her of the sadness and solemnity of the occasion. And so it went.

Needless to say, we were almost immediately in paroxysms of laughter. After a couple of rounds, it was impossible to catch someone's eye and not dissolve again. I remember still being helpless with laughter when it was time to go home.

I didn't think about this episode until I was some way into working on this book. But once I'd remembered it, I suddenly realized that that blissful afternoon of helpless laughter was exactly what I was writing about. The laughter welled up in the midst of a most unpromising situation:

DOI: 10.1057/9781137370914

four little girls, already well acculturated to the expectations of their parents and of society, washed and brushed and dressed in suitable frocks, performing politeness at a tea party. We were constrained by language – or, in a way, by the lack of it: we had not yet learnt the formulae of social interaction. The formality of the game, its ritual and repetitive nature, mimicked and magnified our awkward situation. And yet, at the same time, for no apparent reason, it provoked laughter: magical, unstoppable laughter. What were we laughing at? At our shyness; at our wordlessness; at the rigidities of social convention. At the sudden pleasure of finding a common language in our laughter. At the laughter itself. At everything and nothing. We were released from self-consciousness, and from the need for words. And we laughed.

This is what I would like to call the laughter of delight: a great, irrational, infectious welling-up of joy. It may arise from the most trivial of causes, as well as from the weightiest. It may arise in ordinary or dreary or even hostile situations. The laughter of delight surpasses and baffles language. It dissolves those who laugh it, their presuppositions, their expectations. The laughter of delight is what I am trying to capture in this book, all the while being well aware that it is by its nature uncapturable.

The laughter of delight has been curiously invisible in the copious Western tradition of thinking and writing about laughter: occasionally alluded to, but rarely accorded any philosophical weight. On the one hand, this invisibility is not surprising: Western philosophy has been suspicious of according significance to the disruption of meaning, while Western religion will admit of the aphatic and mystical, but is suspicious of the carnal. The laughter of delight, wherever else it may reach, is inescapably embedded in the carnal, and it certainly disrupts meaning. On the other hand, the invisibility is extraordinary: for arguably the grounding instance of laughter in Judeo-Christian narrative is a laugh of delight, the laughter of Sarah early in the book of Genesis when she gives birth to her son Isaac. This laughter I shall take as the leitmotif of my discussion: the laughter of Sarah as emblematic of the laughter of delight. I shall look at commentary upon it and at commentaries that dodge around it. The laughter of Sarah provides a touchstone for thinking about what the laughter of delight might be and how it might upend our presuppositions about meaning and being.

To begin a book about the laughter of delight with the laughter of children is to begin at its heart. The laughter of children keeps bubbling into the prose of the theorists of laughter, even though it invades and disrupts

DOI: 10.1057/9781137370914

their theories. But I should make clear that this is not some nostalgic project of recuperation. This laughter of delight remains accessible to us; but it (like children, for that matter) has remained largely invisible to Western philosophy or religion.

*    *    *

It is certainly a delight to acknowledge the friends and colleagues in conversation with whom this book was developed. First and foremost, three dear and generous readers. Lisa Saltzman read an early draft and proposed a magnificently fluent re-organization. Jim Crenner and Véronique Pin-Fat read a late one: Jim made the book sleeker, Véro made it tauter. Several other colleagues, among them Lee Burnett, Daniel Caner, Elena Ciletti, Marcia Colish, Gerlinde Huber-Rebenich, Bernard Prusak, Helmut Reimitz, and Bert Roest, will recognize the traces of our conversations – embodied or virtual – and their suggestions; Jim Wetzel, most sympathetic of readers and interlocutors, deserves particular mention. I owe special thanks to the Bryn Mawr graduate students who participated in my seminar on laughter in Spring 2008 and were willing to follow me through so many preliminary divagations and dead ends. I leaned heavily on the guidance of Simon Goldhill, Rachel Havrelock, and – especially – Aryeh Kosman when it came to Hebrew and the rabbinic material; I am still more indebted to Matthew Keegan, who not only advised me on the early Qur'anic commentaries but actually translated them for me. Successive audiences at Berkeley, Cambridge, Bryn Mawr, and Princeton helped me to refine what I wanted to say about laughter; thanks especially to Mary Beard, Peter Brown, and Leslie Kurke for wonderful conversations around those visits.

Finally, there are two dear colleagues with whom I wish the conversation could continue. Fifteen years ago, Grace Jantzen introduced me to her ideas around natality, which I found instantly compelling and which have profoundly influenced this book; she died in 2006. News of the sudden death of Gene Vance erupted into work on a late draft of the manuscript; only a week before, we had been talking about this project, and he had characteristically (and aptly) commanded me to read Kierkegaard's *Fear and Trembling*.

This book, notwithstanding, celebrates life; it is for my son Hilary, who in thirteen years has brought me so much delight.

DOI: 10.1057/9781137370914

palgrave▶**pivot**

www.palgrave.com/pivot

# Introduction: *Ridebat de facto Sara*

Abstract: *This chapter offers a reading of the fifth-century Latin poem, the* Cena Cypriani *(famously used by Umberto Eco in* The Name of the Rose*). The poem is an antic listing of biblical characters attending a feast, each behaving in a way that conforms to their typological characteristics, often to absurd effect; it ends with the words* ridebat de facto Sara, *"Sarah laughed about what had happened." We ask what is special about this laughter, such that it inflects the poem; this introduces the concerns of the book as a whole, and a resumé of its chapters.*

Conybeare, Catherine. *The Laughter of Sarah: Biblical Exegesis, Feminist Theory, and the Concept of Delight.*
New York: Palgrave Macmillan, 2013.
DOI: 10.1057/9781137370914.

Toward the climax of *The Name of the Rose*, Umberto Eco's novel of skull-duggery and erudition in a thirteenth-century monastery, the hapless narrator, Adso, has a dream. The dream is of a chaotic banquet, mixing figures from the Hebrew and Christian scriptures with characters from the monastery, where a succession of grotesque murders has been taking place. The images of the dream grow ever more elaborate and disorienting, until finally Christ is waving his crown of thorns, the Pope is expressing bafflement, and the abbot of the monastery is leading his pigs off to hunt for truffles. It seems merely a florid expression of Adso's fear and exhaustion. But when he confides his dream to his mentor, William of Baskerville, William can readily decode it:

> do you know that to a great extent what you tell me has already been written? You have added people and events of these past few days to a picture already familiar to you, because you have read the story of your dream somewhere, or it was told you as a boy, in school, in the convent. It is the *Coena Cypriani*.[1]

And so it is.

The *Cena Cypriani* is an anonymous poem. It seems to date originally to late antiquity,[2] but it was immensely popular and repeatedly rewritten and re-presented throughout the middle ages.[3] The conceit of the poem is simple, though it is developed to almost impossible degrees of elaboration. A rich roster of biblical characters – and a few from early non-canonical texts – is invited to a dinner party. Each character arrives, is dressed, eats and so on in a way which puns on and literalizes his or her own snippet of biblical narrative. Each characterization is very terse: often only a name and a verb, or a name and a substantive with verb implicit. The figures are ordered according to a playful or perverse web of association within the story of the dinner, not according to their appearance in the biblical narrative, and they may re-appear or disappear as the twisted logic of the tale dictates.

For example, here is the sequence of events when the King Joel, who has convened the banquet, demands that each of the guests help with the preparations before they start to eat:

> First, Elijah looked for fire, Azarias kindled it,
> Jephthah collected the wood, Isaac brought it,
> Joseph chopped it, Jacob uncovered the well,
> Sepphora offered hyssop, Daniel stood by the lake,
> servants brought water, Rebecca a water-jug,

DOI: 10.1057/9781137370914

> Noah proffered wine, Hagar carried a bottle,
> Judas brought silver, Abraham led in a calf,
> Rahab bound it, Jesus offered a net,
> Elijah bound its feet, Peter handed over the knife,
> Daniel crushed it, Cain killed it,
> Habakkuk carried it, Absalom hung it up…
> Rebecca cooked it, Eve tasted it first.[4]

Some of these associations are light-hearted. Joseph, father of Jesus, was a carpenter: who but he should chop the wood? Jacob uncovers the well as a gallant gesture to Rachel, whom he will eventually marry. Jesus' net seems to allude to his desire to make his disciples fishers of men.[5] And Sepphora is one of the midwives who spares the boy-children of the Jews at the beginning of the Exodus story; the hyssop seems to come from the reference to purification with hyssop in the great penitential psalm 51. Some of the associations, although still quite straightforward allusions to biblical stories, are far darker, for they refer to moments of terrible choice or grief or sinfulness. The drunkenness of Noah, the expulsion of Hagar and her son Ishmael into the wilderness to die of thirst and hunger, the betrayal of Christ through the bribing of Judas, Peter's attack on the high priest's servant, Cain's murder of his brother: all are grim stories that here are subsumed into helpful bustling.

But some of the allusions embrace an irony so black as to make one gasp. Jephthah's wood? That's the wood with which he will immolate the sacrifice he has vowed to God as the price of victory in battle – which will turn out to be his own daughter. Isaac, all unawares, brings the wood for his own immolation. Azarias, later called Abednego, was tortured in the fiery furnace – and he brings kindling. Perhaps most painful is the image of Absalom hanging up the slaughtered calf, for Absalom himself is killed on being caught hanging in an oak – and, despite his treachery, is mourned without reserve by his father King David. The darkest allusions are those which mask or mock the fact that, in the biblical narrative, the seemingly harmless motif turns to violence perpetrated against the subject.

This type of compressed, symbolic system of biblical allusion grows and prospers in late antiquity, in both Latin and Greek and across many genres. There is, for example, a version of the sequence above, without the black humor, in a sermon for the newly baptized delivered in the fourth century by Zeno of Verona. He tells them of the heavenly banquet to which they may now look forward: "Christ pours on oil; Moses has

DOI: 10.1057/9781137370914

immediately procured a first-born lamb, and a mature one, Abraham has faithfully procured a fat and established calf; Isaac in his innocence carries a pot and wood." And so on.[6] A variant on the theme, invoking biblical figures as exemplars, is found in the Greek *Apophthegmata Patrum*, the sayings of the desert fathers, which again dates to late antiquity. John the Persian says:

> I have been
>> hospitable like Abraham
>> meek like Moses
>> holy like Aaron
>> patient like Job
>> humble like David
>> a hermit like John
>> filled with compunction like Jeremiah
>> a master like Paul
>> full of faith like Peter
>> wise like Solomon.[7]

But the *Cena Cypriani* is not quite like these. For all that it moves through eating, drinking, after-dinner revelry and antic costumery to a more sombre theme – something is stolen from the feast, and the participants are tortured with their own symbolic accoutrements – it is, in the end, an elaborate joke.

First, its very excesses – its length, its preposterousness – are funny, and are a common device of jokes. (The lines I quoted above constitute only twelve of 289 in Modesto's version of the poem as a whole.) The effect is of watching someone balance along a rather slack high wire. How long can he go on? Can he really add another step? and another? When one section of the high wire is exhausted, the topic changes, and another *tour de force* begins. Second, the succinctness of the individual elements – their abbreviated properties – are also characteristic of jokes, and constitute mini-jokes within the joke of the poem as a whole. The startling juxtapositions, both within the context of the poem and (as we saw above) between the use made of the figures in the poem and their often grave context in the bible, is part of the effect. So is the sing-song rhythm set up in each section. To give a sense of the effect, I shall quote an example in Latin. The passage describes where each of the company chooses to sit: "Adam in medio, Eva super folia,/ Cain super aratrum, Abel super mulgarium,/ Noe super archam, Iaphet super lateres,/ Abraham sub arbore, Isaac super aram,/ Iacob super petram, Loth iuxta

DOI: 10.1057/9781137370914

ostium,/ Moyses super lapidem, Helias super pellem…" and so on. This sort of rhythm, and the absurdist compression that drives it, seems to resonate in schoolyard jokes and rhymes down the centuries.[8]

Much of the humor smacks of the schoolyard too. This certainly applies to the casual brutality, to which I have already drawn attention, but also to moments of glorious literalism – Eve sits on a pile of leaves, Ruth, the first gleaner, on corn-stubble – or of inspired scatology: at the end of the description of the seating arrangements, "and Job was sad, because he was the only one sitting in shit." We may also note the near-blasphemous brinksmanship: for example, amid the list of tortures after the theft from the banqueting hall, Jesus is casually crucified, just one among many.

But there is one element above all that seems to secure and predict our response to the poem: its conclusion. This is an element not mentioned in Eco's re-working of the poem for Adso's dream, which ends, as I mentioned, with the abbot and his pigs looking for truffles. The anonymous author writes:

> Zachariah cried out for joy at what had happened,
> Elizabeth was confounded, Mary was astounded,
> Sarah laughed about it.

Sarah laughed about it: *ridebat de facto Sara.* Each of these four typologically-linked figures[9] respond in a characteristic way; but by placing Sarah's laughter at the end – inverting the biblical chronology – and using the near-redundant phrase *de facto*, which could mean "about the deed" or, more comprehensively, "about what had happened," the author seems to suggest that this is the most appropriate response.[10] Sarah has the last word – only it isn't a word, it's a laugh. Her laughter upstages even the astonished response of Mary, the mother of Christ. The laughter of Sarah seems to ripple back across the poem, and to suggest a way to "read" the poem.

On one level, this laughter seems a proper response to the absurdities of the *Cena Cypriani*, to its sublime crazy logic.[11] The poem vaunts so many of the age-old topoi of humor. But the laughter of Sarah runs deeper: it celebrates the glorious excess of invention in the poem, and its near-blasphemy – especially in the re-situating of exemplary figures in the corporeal world. This glorious corporeal excess opens out from the attention bestowed by the *Cena* on the letter of the biblical portrayal. It also shows, quite simply, that laughter is the primary association with the figure of Sarah.

DOI: 10.1057/9781137370914

This is a book about that laughter, and the glorious corporeal excess that goes along with it. Despite the setup, this is not a book about jokes: their dynamics have long been amply analyzed and discussed. It is a book about laughter: the very moment of laughter, what it means to try to capture it, what it means to read through it. Further, it is about the laughter of delight: the laughter that wells up in Sarah when she gives birth to Isaac, what I called in the prelude a great, irrational, infectious welling-up of joy. This type of laughter seems to me to have been largely overlooked by the Western interpretative tradition – and yet here, at the heart of both Jewish and Christian scripture, is the powerful image of a joyously laughing woman. In the course of this book, I reflect upon the epistemological and ontological challenge of this laughter, and on the consequences of engaging with it. What does the laughter of Sarah enable? What does it release? How might it change what we see, and how we understand it?

After reading the episode of Genesis from which my book takes its title, I consider the laughter of Sarah in the light of three bodies of work. The first is the commentaries on the laughter of Sarah from late antiquity – from roughly the second to the fifth centuries CE – whether in Greek, Latin, or Hebrew. Both Christian and Jewish traditions are represented here; I also look briefly at early commentaries on the Qur'an in which, although she is not named, Sarah still laughs. The second is the work of four major theorists of laughter of the twentieth century, Henri Bergson, Sigmund Freud, Mikhail Bakhtin, and Helmuth Plessner. The third is a range of contemporary theoretical work that can be related to the philosophical problems raised by the laughter of delight, and that serves as inspiration and stimulus to my own observations about the significance of laughter.

The late antique commentaries perhaps require a little more explanation here. It seems to me that they have been crucial in shaping the responses to Sarah's laughter – and, by extension, to laughter more generally – over the centuries. Little is added in later medieval interpretation: hence my constant recurrence to the early commentaries as part of my frame of reference here.[12] For Jewish commentary, I turn to Midrash, the compendious and polyphonic commentary by the rabbis compiled some time in the fifth century. Philo will also be very important in this work: he is one of our earliest commentators, flourishing as he did in the first century; although he too is Jewish, his commentaries are not (proto-)rabbinical, but inaugurate a neo-

DOI: 10.1057/9781137370914

Platonic reading of the Hebrew scriptures. This type of reading is then taken up by the Alexandrians, a group of Christian interpreters of the second century writing in Greek – most notably, for my purposes, the bishop Clement of Alexandria and the brilliant but "heretical" Origen – and by some Latin writers too, notably Ambrose, bishop of Milan in the fourth century. Of fourth-century Greek interpreters, by far the most significant here is John Chrysostom, who was archbishop of Constantinople; of the Latin interpreters, the most significant are the North African Augustine, bishop of Hippo, and Jerome, monk and presbyter of Bethlehem.

Aristotle pointed out, in typically lapidary fashion, that laughter is unique to humanity (though we may note that, despite the significant legacy of his observation, it was originally made as part of an analysis of tickling[13]). In the late second century CE, Clement of Alexandria brought Aristotle into the nascent tradition of Christian thought, saying that laughter was one of the things "natural to humankind (*physika tois anthrōpois*)."[14] Medieval thinkers seem to have taken the claim further: the twelfth-century scholar Peter Abelard proposes a syllogism containing the term *si aliquis est homo, ipse est risibilis*: "if someone is a human being, that same person is laughable" – or "capable of laughter."[15] Versions of these claims have been remarkably consistent across time and in the face of attempts to depose them.[16]

I should also mention that practically every great thinker of the modern period has had his (it is almost invariably his) say on the subject of laughter. Hobbes situated it in a sudden sense of superiority;[17] Baudelaire identified it with the demonic;[18] Kierkegaard, Nietzsche, Schopenhauer, even Kafka, and many more contribute their thoughts and have been interpreted and re-interpreted in their turn.[19] I shall not attempt to discuss them all in the course of the book, though each may at different stages have inflected my commentary.

In chapters 1 and 2, I give an account of the biblical episode of Sarah's laughter and then look systematically at late antique exegesis of that episode in the Greek and Latin Christian traditions; in the Jewish tradition, represented by Philo (writing in Greek) and by the rabbinic interpretation of Midrash; and, briefly, at exegesis in the tradition of early Quranic interpretation. Chapter 1 looks at biblical interpretation *ad litteram*, "according to the letter," which seeks meaning in the immediate narrative; chapter 2 looks at typological or allegorical interpretations of the episode, in which it is read as pointing elsewhere, to symbolic meaning

DOI: 10.1057/9781137370914

or to the end times. Chapters 3 and 4 focus primarily on the four great theorists of laughter, Bergson, Freud, Bakhtin, and Plessner, and consider their ideas with reference specifically to the laughter of delight: I group Bergson and Freud together in chapter 3, under the loose notion of theorists concerned with power dynamics in laughter, and Bakhtin and Plessner, who elucidate the relationship of laughter to the body and to embodied experience, in chapter 4.

The book's principal theoretical contribution comes in chapters 5, 6, and 7, in which I focus on the epistemological and ontological significance of the laughter of delight. In these chapters, I take my inspiration from a network of ideas loosely grouped around the Arendtian notion of "natality"[20] – ideas that include, for example, Julia Kristeva's early work on the "semiotic" and the insistence of Adriana Cavarero and Luce Irigaray on immanence, process, and the embodied experience of language – and from a philosophical resistance to universalization that can be traced back to Wittgenstein. Chapter 5 explores the consequences of laughter's fundamentally embodied nature; chapter 6 looks at the relation of the laughter of delight to language; chapter 7, at its relationship to time. Over these three chapters, I develop a picture of laughter as necessarily embodied, radically unstable, unreproducible, resistant to representation, and peculiarly situated in time; I use this picture to destabilize a conventional notion of language, communication, and the construction of meaning, and to question conventional ontology. The laughter of delight is read as an instant of radical openness that explodes the teleological tendencies of interpretation.

Let us consider, then, this laughter which rings so powerfully through time, and yet which draws attention to the immediacy of communication and to the specificity of the bodily moment: the laughter of delight, the laughter of Sarah.

# Notes

1   Eco, U. *The Name of the Rose* tr. William Weaver (London: Secker & Warburg, 1983), 437.
2   Glei, R. F. "Ridebat de facto Sarra. Bemerkungen zur *Cena Cypriani*", in *Literaturparodie in Antike und Mittelalter* ed. W. Ax and R. F. Glei, 153–70 (Trier: Bochumer Altertumswissenschaftliches Colloquium 15, 1993), calls it a typical fourth century *exercitium ingenii*.

DOI: 10.1057/9781137370914

3  For a century, the best edition was that by Strecker in the *Monumenta Germaniae Historica* – stranded in a Carolingian volume, because Hrabanus Maurus had written a version of the poem which was Strecker's main editorial focus. Christine Modesto has now sorted through the convolutions of the manuscripts and produced a new edition, with limited commentary.

4  Modesto, C. *Studien zur* Cena Cypriani *und zu deren Rezeption*, Classica Monacensia 3 (Tübingen: Gunter Narr Verlag, 1992), 20, lines 1–18, omitting lines 12–17.

5  *Pace* Modesto, who associates *resticulam porrexit Iesus* with Mark 15:1 and the binding of Christ before he is taken to Pilate; but *resticulam* is more naturally taken as a net, not bonds, hence my invocation of Mark 1:17.

6  Zeno of Verona, *Tractatus* ed. B. Löfstedt, CCL 22 (Turnhout 1971), I.24 (II.38 in PL numeration). Note the allusions to the new – Christian – covenant in Moses' "mature" lamb and Abraham's "established" calf, procured with faith (*fideliter*). Further precursors to the *Cena Cypriani* are listed in both Glei, "Ridebat de facto Sarra," and Mosetti Casaretto, F. "Modelli e antimodelli per la 'Cena Cypriani': il 'teatro interiore', Zenone e…Apuleio!" *Wiener Studien* 119 (2006), 215–46.

7  *Apophthegmata Patrum*, John the Persian 4 (PG 65, cols. 237–40); quoted in Krueger, D. "The Old Testament in Monasticism," in *The Old Testament in Byzantium*, ed. Paul Magdalino and Robert Nelson (Washington DC: Dumbarton Oaks, 2010), 199–221, in which see also Krueger's discussion of the dynamics of biblical exemplarity.

8  See e.g. Opie, I. and Opie, P. *The Lore and Language of Schoolchildren* (Oxford: Oxford University Press, 1959); Lerer, S. *Children's Literature: A Reader's History, from Aesop to Harry Potter* (Chicago and London: University of Chicago Press, 2008) ch. 3; Orme, N. "Children and Literature in Medieval England," *Medium Aevum* 68 (1999), 218–46.

9  See further, chapter 1.

10 So too Glei, though he seems appalled by "das blasphemische Lachen Saras."

11 See Huizinga, J. *Homo Ludens: A Study of the Play Element in Culture* (Boston: Beacon Press, 1950; first published in German, 1944), ch. 1, on the "freedom" characteristic of play.

12 To pursue medieval thought on laughter, one could start with Curtius' marvellous Excursus, "Jest and Earnest in Medieval Literature," *European Literature and the Latin Middle Ages* tr. W. Trask (London: Routledge and Kegan Paul, 1953; new ed. with afterword by P. Godman, Princeton: Princeton University Press, 1990; first published in German, 1948), 417–35, and then look at the essays in Halsall, G. (ed.) *Humour, History and Politics in Late Antiquity and the Early Middle Ages* (Cambridge: Cambridge University Press, 2002), and Braet, H., G. Latré, and W. Verbeke, *Risus Mediaevalis: Laughter in Medieval Literature and Art* (Leuven: Leuven University Press,

DOI: 10.1057/9781137370914

2003), or a summary work such as Minois, G. *Histoire du rire et de la dérision* (Paris: Fayard, 2000).

13    "That a human being alone is affected by tickling is due first to the delicacy of its skin, and second *to its being the only animal that laughs*," *De Partibus Animalium* 3.10, 673a8.

14    Clement of Alexandria, *Paedagogus I-III* ed. H.-I. Marrou, SC 70, 108, 158 (Paris 1960, 1965, 1970), II.5.46.1; on Clement's treatment of laughter, see Halliwell, S. *Greek Laughter: a Study in Cultural Psychology from Homer to Early Christianity* (Cambridge: Cambridge University Press, 2008), 483–95.

15    Abelard, *Dialectica,* 319 (de Rijk edition). Further examples in Adolf, H. "On Mediaeval Laughter," *Speculum* 22 (1947), 251–3, building on Tatlock, J. S. P. "Mediaeval Laughter," *Speculum* 21 (1946), 289–94.

16    It is conventional at this point to pursue the question of whether animals laugh – see Douglas, M. "Do Dogs Laugh?" in eadem, *Implicit Meanings: Essays in Anthropology* (London: Routledge and Paul, 1975), and R. R. Provine's work on laughter ("There is a common misperception that laughter is exclusive to human beings," "Laughter," *American Scientist* 84:1 [1996] 40). But this is not relevant to my project, above all because of the connections I draw between laughter and epistemology.

17    In both *Leviathan* and *Human Nature*; see Skinner, Q. "Hobbes and the classical theory of laughter," in idem, *Visions of Politics* vol. 3 (Cambridge: Cambridge University Press, 2002), 142–76, and my brief discussion at the beginning of chapter 3.

18    See Baudelaire, C. "De l'essence du rire, et généralement du comique dans les arts plastiques," in Baudelaire, *Oeuvres complètes* ed. C. Pichois (Paris: Gallimard, 1975), 2: 525–43.

19    See e.g. J. Lippitt's invaluable overview articles in *Cogito*, and his "Nietzsche, Zarathustra and the Status of Laughter," *British Journal of Aesthetics* 32 (1992), 39–49; S. Kierkegaard's *Fear and Trembling* tr. H. and E. Hong, Kierkegaard's Writings VI (Princeton, NJ: Princeton University Press, 1983; first published in Swedish, 1843); Higgins, K. M. "Waves of Uncountable Laughter," in *Nietzsche's Futures* ed. J. Lippitt (Basingstoke: MacMillan, 1999), 82–98; Sternstein, M. "Laughter, Gesture, and Flesh: Kafka's 'In the Penal Colony'," *Modernism/modernity* 8 (2001), 315–23.

20    Developed in Arendt, H. *The Human Condition* intr. M. Canovan (Chicago: University of Chicago Press, 1998; first published 1958); see my discussion in Conybeare, C. *The Irrational Augustine* (Oxford: Oxford University Press, 2006), 195–202: "Augustine amongst the natals."

DOI: 10.1057/9781137370914

# 1
# Sarah in the Bible: A Peculiar Laugh

Abstract: *Here, we read the biblical narrative of Sarah's laughter at the birth of Isaac, as well as the two immediately preceding instances of laughter in the book of Genesis, the anxious and doubting laughs of Sarah and her husband Abraham when they are told that they are going to have a late-born son. We then look at biblical commentaries from late antiquity – both Jewish and Christian, as well as early commentary on the Qur'an – that respond to this laughter* ad litteram, *according to a literal interpretation, to show the difficulty which they have in "hearing" the second, delighted, laugh of Sarah.*

Conybeare, Catherine. *The Laughter of Sarah: Biblical Exegesis, Feminist Theory, and the Concept of Delight.* New York: Palgrave Macmillan, 2013.
DOI: 10.1057/9781137370914.

The laughter of Sarah, and of Abraham her husband, is the first laughter we hear in Jewish scripture; and hence, it is the first we hear in Christian scripture too.

There are three moments of laughter, each utterly individual. They are embedded in a story of suffering and displacement and almost unbearable belatedness.[1] God has promised Abraham that he will be the father and forefather of multitudes; but the couple wait and wait, and no children come.

Sarah and Abraham were originally called Sarai and Abram. They are old. Although God has promised them heirs, Sarai is ninety and Abram is a hundred and they have long despaired of having children of their own. Some fourteen years before, in fact, Sarai sent Abram to have a child with her Egyptian servant woman, Hagar, who duly conceived.

Sarai resented Hagar's impending motherhood and sent Hagar away. An angel stopped Hagar on her way back home to Egypt and urged her to humility, and promised her countless descendents. Hagar returned and gave birth to Ishmael, whom Abram brought up as his son.

The biblical account is spare; but it leaves the reader in little doubt of the tensions between this interlaced trio. In a household that must in fact have been numerous, we meet only Abram, Sarai, and Hagar, standing out in sharp relief, and we feel the heat of their anguished encounters.[2] This is not fertile ground for laughter.

At this point, God makes another promise. He changes Abram's name to Abraham and Sarai's to Sarah, interposing the Hebrew consonant *Hē*, as a sign of God's covenant with Abraham and his descendents; and he enjoins upon Abraham and all his descendents the rite of circumcision. But this is not all. In Robert Alter's incomparable translation from the Hebrew:

> And God said to Abraham, "Sarai your wife shall no longer call her name Sarai, for Sarah is her name. And I will bless her and I will also give you from her a son and I will bless him, and she shall become nations, kings of peoples shall issue from her." And Abraham flung himself on his face and he laughed, saying to himself,
> "To a hundred-year-old will a child be born,
>     will ninety-year-old Sarah give birth?" (Gen. 17:15–17)

Abraham's laughter seems to be that of bafflement and disbelief, and perhaps amusement at the absurdity of the idea, even though the announcement comes from God; he deflects the blessing onto his son Ishmael: "Would that Ishmael might live in your favor!" But God insists that a

DOI: 10.1057/9781137370914

new child will come – "Yet Sarah your wife is to bear you a son" – and his name is to be Isaac. Isaac means, in Hebrew, "he will laugh."

Sarah's first laugh is disbelieving, too. Three men – who are, or who represent, God – visit Abraham as he sits at his tent flap in Mamre.

> And they said to him, "Where is Sarah your wife?" And he said, "There, in the tent." And he said, "I will surely return to you at this very season and, look, a son shall Sarah your wife have," and Sarah was listening at the tent flap, which was behind him. And Abraham and Sarah were old, advanced in years, Sarah no longer had her woman's flow. And Sarah laughed inwardly, saying, "After being shriveled, shall I have pleasure, and my husband is old?" And the Lord said to Abraham, "Why is it that Sarah laughed, saying, 'Shall I really give birth, old as I am?' Is anything beyond the Lord? In due time I will return to you, at this very season, and Sarah shall have a son." And Sarah dissembled, saying, "I did not laugh," for she was afraid. And He said, "Yes, you did laugh." (Gen. 18:9–15)

Sarah's laugh betrays a rich sense of the absurd: this birth is impossible. It seems a laugh fitted to the occasion. But God's response marks it out as disbelieving: "Is anything beyond the Lord?"

Apparently not:

> And the Lord singled out Sarah as He had said, and the Lord did for Sarah as He had spoken. And Sarah conceived and bore a son to Abraham in his old age at the set time that God had spoken to him. And Abraham called the name of his son who was born to him, whom Sarah bore him, Isaac. And Abraham circumcised Isaac his son when he was eight days old, as God had commanded him. And Abraham was a hundred years old when Isaac his son was born to him. And Sarah said,
>
> "Laughter has God made me,
>     Whoever hears will laugh with me."
>
> And she said,
>
> "Who would have uttered to Abraham –
>     'Sarah is suckling sons!'
>         For I have borne a son in his old age." (Gen. 21:1–7)

This is a moment of exuberant delight. Is Sarah actually laughing? Commentators ancient and modern have assumed so – helped by the fact that in Greek or Latin Sarah's first exclamation is simply, "God has made laughter for me." The whole narrative leading up to the birth of Isaac rings with laughter. It seems to me that here the biblical narrator stands back and allows Sarah herself to announce her dissolution into laughter.

DOI: 10.1057/9781137370914

She is consumed with laughter; she has become laughter: "Laughter has God made me." But God has also made laughter *for* her: both her son, Isaac, "he will laugh"; and the laughter itself, which expresses all the joy of the unexpected birth and the release from anxiety and grief and despair. The laughter is infectious, as laughter is prone to be: this delight is not solipsistic, it bursts forth, drawing in everyone who hears it with its joy.

At the same time, this laughter has a complicated undertow. Its richness is of darkness as well as delight. Sarah is aware that she is conspicuous: "Sarah is suckling sons!" Her conspicuousness may cause mockery as well as delight. The phrase "whoever hears will laugh with me" may also be translated "will laugh *at* me."[3] Sarah is exultant, but her laughter is not simple, not least in acknowledging that others' laughter may erupt as well, and it may have an edge. Each laugh is peculiar, unique, complex, and bound up in every other one.

Sarah's laugh of delight is deeply inflected by her laugh of disbelief, and her husband's laugh of disbelief as well, and that of all the other possible people laughing; and yet it is still the laughter of delight, of joy, and it resonates back through her disbelief and forward into the other great exultant moments of birth in the Bible.[4] Hannah rejoices like this when she dedicates her long-awaited son Samuel to God in the temple. This time the laughter finds words: her prayer of joy, exultation, defiance, and humility before God articulates and yet does not complete the consuming laughter of Sarah. Mary rejoices like this when she visits her cousin Elisabeth, once barren, now with child: the miraculous pregnancies of Sarah and Elisabeth are linked by the repeated phrase "For with God nothing shall be impossible" (Luke 1:37 and Genesis 18:14). Mary's joy finds expression in the Magnificat (Luke 1:46–55). But perhaps it is Elisabeth's baby who most fully expresses delight, for he "leaps in her womb": Elisabeth says, "As soon as ever the voice of thy greeting sounded in my ears, the child in my womb leaped for joy." We can imagine him, who will become John the Baptist, exclaiming, "Laughter has God made me."

So the first laugh of delight in Jewish and Christian scripture is the laugh of an old, old woman who has given birth to a son. She knows she is old, she knows this is absurd and impossible, and she laughs. And the son himself is named in commemoration as Isaac, "he will laugh." It is in this moment of delight that I wish to dwell for the remainder of this book.

\*   \*   \*

DOI: 10.1057/9781137370914

The first Christian commentators on scripture worked in a context notoriously hostile to laughter.[5] It was pointed out very early on that the gospels contain no account of Jesus laughing, and this became something of a leitmotif in early Christian sources.[6] Indeed, the insistence of early Christian writers on the subject seems to betray a deep anxiety about laughter, animated on the one hand by fear of identification with the Jews who purportedly mocked Christ on the cross,[7] and on the other by fear of being tainted with Gnosticism. Gnosticism told the story of a last-minute substitution of Christ on the cross: Christ himself ascended instantly to heaven and sat by his father laughing at the travails of the dying mortals below him.[8] No wonder laughter was a source of anxiety.

This anxiety is reflected in the treatment of laughter in Clement of Alexandria's *Paedagogus*, written around 200 CE, which advises the Christian on how to comport himself in the world. Clement devotes a section of the *Paedagogus* specifically to laughter – sandwiching it, revealingly, between a discussion on how to behave at banquets and a treatment of *aischrologia*, shameful speech – and though he admits that laughter is "natural," he is mostly concerned with constraining and delimiting it (*Paed.* II.5.46). That theme continues in the *Rules* for the regulation of monastic life compiled by Basil of Caesarea in the 360s CE.[9] When Basil takes on the topic of laughter, it is not surprising, given a context of asceticism, that he views it with suspicion, since for Basil, bursting into laughter tends to show a lack of self-control. He too repeats the time-honored motif that "our Lord never laughed." All the same, he warns, "Let the ambiguity (*homōnymia*) of laughter not mislead us." The simple term "laughter" (in Greek, *gelōs*) can refer to different types of effusion – and they do not necessarily involve the loss of self-control that Basil finds obnoxious. He gives three instances from the Bible of acceptable laughter: the consolation of Bildad to Job, "[God] will fill a truthful mouth with laughter" (Job 8:21); the ultimate laughter of the beatitudes, "blessed are those who weep now, for they shall laugh" (Luke 6:21), of which we shall hear more in chapter 2;[10] and – first in Basil's order, as in the biblical chronology – the laughter of Sarah, in Greek *gelōta moi epoiēsen ho Theos*, "God has made laughter for me." All these instances of laughter, these uses of *gelōs*, says Basil, express "instead of frivolous gaiety (*hilarotēs*)[11], spiritual exultation (*hē kata psychēn agalliasis*)." *Agalliasis*, "exultation," is a word first used in the Septuagint, the second-century BCE translation of the Hebrew scriptures into Greek. (My Greek dictionary glosses it, rather sweetly, as "exceeding great joy.") It seems to

DOI: 10.1057/9781137370914

capture exactly the sense of explosive, exalted delight that we hear in the laughter of Sarah.

So the word "laughter" is ambiguous, as Basil tells us. Indeed, we need a term fuller than "ambiguous," which in its origins only suggests a spanning of two possible meanings: we need something that embraces the many possibilities inherent in the notion of laughter. Clearly, even a thinker as invested as Basil in outlawing laughter can mark the occasional excellent instance of laughter. Clearly too, the so-called fathers of the church will be deeply invested in the interpretation of Genesis, and hence will be confronted with the laughter of Sarah. What do they make of her exuberant laughter? Is it always *agalliasis*? And what of the laughter that precedes it?

Sometimes, the solution is simply to pass over the laughter in silence. One of the earliest Christian interpretations of Genesis, Origen's second-century *Homilies on Genesis* – available, admittedly, only in the fourth-century translation into Latin of Rufinus – does not mention it: the biblical account is simply reported as, "And Sarah your wife will have a son. Sarah heard, as she stood behind the opening of her tent, behind Abraham." *Post ostium tabernaculi sui post Abraham*: note the repeated *post*, "behind": Origen's moral becomes that a man should go first to God, and a woman should follow.[12] In his homily on the nativity of Isaac, Origen simply says, "Isaac means laughter or joy" (*Isaac risus vel gaudium interpretatur: Hom. in Gen.* 7.1), and then turns his attention to the weaning of Isaac and its allegorical interpretations.

Two centuries later, Gregory of Nazianzus composed a set of poems obsessively writing and re-writing the epitaphs for his parents. He repeatedly likens his mother, Nonna, to Sarah. In one of these epitaphs, indeed, he compares her to both Sarah and Hannah:

> Wise Sarah revered her beloved husband; but you, mother, made your good husband first a Christian, then a great priest...Hannah, you prayed and gave birth to a beloved son, then you gave him to the temple – the meek servant Samuel...Nonna won the glory of both.[13]

It is always Sarah's devotion to her husband and son that Gregory emphasizes; her laughter is never mentioned.

Other commentators do, however, attempt to engage Sarah's laughter. Consider the subtly varying interpretations of Augustine. In his *Questions on Genesis,* Augustine poses the question of why God criticized Sarah's laughter, "since Abraham laughed too. Except that his was the laughter

DOI: 10.1057/9781137370914

of wonder and delight, but Sarah's the laughter of doubt – and He who knows the hearts of men could discriminate between the two." In that case, how could Sarah have dared to deny that she had laughed? "Perhaps because Sarah thought that they [the visitors at Mamre] were men, while Abraham understood that they were God" (*quaest. Gen.* 36, 37). This divided response seems at first to be found too in Augustine's most extensive treatment of Abraham and Sarah, in the *City of God.* Augustine explains, "The laughter of Abraham is the exultation of the joyful, not the derision of the faithless (*risus Abrahae exultatio est gratulantis, non inrisio diffidentis*). And those words in his own heart, 'Shall a son be born to me, being one hundred? Shall Sarah, being ninety, give birth?' are those not of doubt but of wonder (*non...dubitantis, sed admirantis*)" (*civ.* 16.26). At this point, Augustine makes no reference to Sarah's laughter. But later on, he explains the name Isaac, "which means laughter":

> For his father had laughed when [the child] was promised to him, in won-
> dering joy; and his mother had laughed too, when [the child] was promised
> again through those three men, in doubtful joy. The angel reproached her
> that her laughter, even if it was joyful, was not the laughter of complete faith;
> but afterwards, she was confirmed in her faith by that same angel.... For
> once Isaac had been born, and called by that name, Sarah showed that that
> laughter pertained not to risible shame, but to joyful celebration, for she
> said, "Laughter has the Lord made for me...." (*civ.* 16.31)[14]

In this reading, Sarah's second burst of laughter somehow validates, or else simply cancels out, her first, apparently ambivalent one.

Consider further the readings of the laughter of Abraham and Sarah provided by Ambrose of Milan. In a letter to a fellow-bishop (the same letter in which he celebrates the conspicuous ascetic retreat of Paulinus of Nola and his wife), he demands, "Could one think what God commanded was shameful? Because Sarah laughed, she was convicted of disbelief, while Abraham was praised because he did not hesitate at the word of God, and was given the highest reward, because with God's command he believed he could even become a pious murderer" (*ep.* 6.27.14). Clearly the context, approving a man's notionally immediate, unhesitating obedience to God, has driven the interpretation, which is facilitated by Ambrose' silence about Abraham's laughter. For as we have seen, Abraham did hesitate: he laughed, he thought of his excessive age, and in his hesitation he deflected God's promise onto Ishmael. Only in response to the command to sacrifice Isaac did Abraham not hesitate.

DOI: 10.1057/9781137370914

The first part of Ambrose's treatise *On Abraham* gives us a set of unabashedly updated readings of the episode.[15] (I shall read the second part in the next chapter, for reasons which will become apparent.) He is preoccupied simultaneously with interpreting the text, proving that it applies to the Christian inheritance not (just) to the Jewish, and proving – still further – that it applies to Christians today. His view is very much that from the prosperous suburbs: wives should not be jealous; husbands should not marry out of their class; husbands should always choose wives who are in no respect superior to them – for husbands must always lead.

Ambrose's anti-Jewish agenda is apparent when he narrates God's promise to Abraham of Isaac's birth. It's important, he says, that Isaac was promised *before* the covenant of circumcision – this shows that Abraham is 'father' to all believers, not just (not at all?) to the Jews. He adds, giving almost exactly the same interpretation as Augustine would later provide, "That Abraham laughed when the son was promised was a sign not of disbelief, but of exultation" (*Ab.* 1.4.31).

Ambrose is more generous to Sarah here than in his letter: "But Sarah laughed. Think of this as an indication, not of disbelief, but of what was to come. For she laughed, although she still didn't know why she was laughing, because she was going to give birth to public delight in (the form of) Isaac (*quod publicam esset in Isaac paritura laetitiam*). So she denied that she had laughed, because she didn't know; but she laughed, because she was foretelling it" (*Ab.* 1.5.43). Again in his *Exhortation to Virginity*, when Ambrose is discouraging his virginal audience from laughter in the context of a discussion of the terrible laughter of the foolish at Christ on the cross: "Sarah was right to deny that she had laughed, lest by laughing she might seem to have doubted the efficacy of heavenly promises; and yet that laughter was full of seriousness and modesty, laughter which no witness knew about except God, who is aware of hidden things" (*ex. virg.* 11.76). When we start talking about the "seriousness and modesty" (*gravitas et pudor*) of a moment of laughter, we may well wonder exactly what sort of laughter this is. Time and again, the fathers of the church, however engaged they may try to be, dodge away from Sarah's laughter. They do not want to hear it. There is something embarrassing about the laughter of Sarah. It is too intense, too loud, out of place even in a story rife with passion and disruption.

Of the Christian interpreters in late antiquity, John Chrysostom – the "golden-mouthed" fourth-century archbishop of Constantinople, exiled

DOI: 10.1057/9781137370914

and disgraced but always renowned for his preaching – is the only one who is truly willing to listen to Sarah's laughter. Chrysostom's account of Abraham's feelings as he prepared to sacrifice Isaac can make you weep in a library on a perfectly ordinary afternoon. It is no surprise, then, that he provides the most sympathetic and personal account of the laughter of both Abraham and Sarah. Abraham "fell on his face and laughed" at the promise of a son not because he didn't believe, but because he didn't have anything to say (*ouk echōn ho ti eipēi*); he was, in fact, at a loss, "panic-stricken" (*kataplageis*) at God's promise (*Hom. in Gen.* 40.1; col. 370). On Sarah's laughter, Chrysostom points out that scripture excuses her because of her age. And besides, Sarah was merely "thinking to herself"; so in "hearing" this silent laughter, God reveals himself: he knows what is hidden.

God can also perform the impossible: "I can bring a dead womb to life, and make it fit [for birth]" (*Hom. in Gen.* 41.6; col. 383). Indeed, "my word will be inviolable (*aparabaton*)." Chrysostom seems less at ease with Sarah's laughter here: he passes over it swiftly, it is prefaced by a passage against womanly excess, and the conclusion of the sermon exhorts the congregation to hospitality and its everlasting rewards. The delight of good works is the "joyous mind" (*gnōmē hilara*).

Chrysostom's rendition of Sarah's delight at Isaac's birth, however, shows no embarrassment (*Hom in Gen.* 45). He glosses the specificity of the phrase "whom Sarah bore to him": "that is, the sterile woman, the childless one, the aged one." That puts into context his commentary on her laughter over Isaac. The translation from the Hebrew which I used above captures an original ambiguity – even ambivalence – in Sarah's moment of celebration as "Laughter has God made me." But the Septuagint, which Chrysostom is using, seems to me far less ambiguous: *Gelōta moi epoiēsen ho Kurios*, "the Lord has made laughter for me"; at its weakest, that *moi* would be an ethic dative, which is the grammatical case used to express some unspecified state of interest or reference to the subject. Chrysostom attempts to translate Sarah's laughter into words:

> The child is a subject of delight for me. And what is to be wondered at, that it should be so "for me"? And I shall have all those who hear me as sharers in my joy, not because I gave birth, but because I gave birth in this way (*houtōs*). The paradox of the birth will stun everyone into wonder, when they learn that I who was no better than the dead have in an instant (*athroon*) become a mother, and from a lifeless womb I gave birth to a child, and

DOI: 10.1057/9781137370914

> I can even suckle [him], and I who had no remaining hope of childbirth can release fountains of milk. (*Hom. in Gen.* 45.5: col. 421)

It is the *houtōs*, "in this way," that is revealing. This gives us the specificity of the occasion for laughter, all the circumstances of the aged and sterile body at whose sudden overflowing fertility Sarah expresses delight. Suddenly, "in an instant" (*athroon*), all the exuberant delight of an unexpected, unhoped for, despaired of birth overflows. This is the laughter that God has made for Sarah, at the age of ninety: the public joy, the social restitution, the breasts brimming with milk that prove the child is truly hers.

This frankness about the corporeal delight that Sarah feels, and expresses in her laughter, is unparalleled in the general run of Christian commentary. But we hear it richly echoed in Midrash, the compendious, polyphonic biblical commentary developed by the rabbis in late antiquity.[16] The rabbis are particularly concerned with the gush of milk that proves Sarah's belated motherhood. Even at the prophecy to Abraham in Gen. 17:16, R. Judah glosses the double blessing as bespeaking two separate phases of Sarah's miraculous childbearing: "*And I will bless her*, that she should give thee a son; *yea, I will bless her* in respect of milk." In the questioning that follows, the milk is clearly linked with Sarah's renewed youth and her incipient fertility (Midrash Rabbah 47.2). The same connections are made when Isaac is born: "R. Judah expounded: *And the Lord remembered Sarah* – to give her a son; *And the Lord did unto Sarah as He had spoken* – to bless her with milk" (MR 53.5). The culmination of the rabbinic emphasis on Sarah's milk comes in as a gloss on Sarah's second ecstatic exclamation,

> "Who would have uttered to Abraham –
>     'Sarah is suckling sons!'"

"Our mother Sarah" – say the rabbis – "was extremely modest. Said Abraham to her: 'This is not a time for modesty, but uncover your breasts so that all may know that the Holy One, blessed be He, has begun to perform miracles.' She uncovered her breasts and the milk gushed forth as from two fountains, and noble ladies came and had their children suckled by her, saying, 'We do not merit that our children should be suckled with the milk of that righteous woman'. The Rabbis said: Whoever came for the sake of heaven became God-fearing" (MR 53.9). Abraham urges his wife to move from modest concealment to disclosure: from appropriate deportment to something radically inappropriate. Yet this inappropriate

DOI: 10.1057/9781137370914

moment has been commanded and precipitated by God. The mocking disclosure celebrates God's omnipresence – "for with God, all things are possible." Further, the stark image of the uncovering of Sarah's breasts seems to parallel the stark uncovering of her emotions that is about to be displayed in her eruptive laughter.

What of Sarah's actual laughter in Midrash? The interpretation is complicated; but so is the Hebrew word for laughter. The semantic range of *tsehoq*, which means laughter, is far broader than that of the Greek *gelōs* or even the Latin *risus* (which may also mean "smile"). The laughter expressed by *tsehoq* may be negative, aggressive, mocking, as well as jubilant. It may be simply playful. It may also be the laughter that accompanies sexual teasing and flirtation – remember that Sarah has asked, "Shall I have pleasure (*'ednah*), and my husband is old?"[17] The association with sex and flirtation is clear when, later in Genesis, Abimelech catches sight of Isaac "laughing" with Rebecca, his wife (Gen. 26:8); it appears with a doubtful sinister cast when Sarah sees Ishmael "laughing" after Isaac's birth (in many translations of Genesis, it is specified that he is laughing *with Isaac*, though as Jerome points out, "it's not in the Hebrew"[18]),which leads her once again to drive away Ishmael and his mother, Hagar (Gen. 21:9).[19]

When Sarah first laughs, the rabbis report an emendation: she laughed not "inwardly," but "before her relatives": her challenge to God's prophecy is thereby made public, not like Abraham's private response (his laughter is incidentally not reported in this version of Midrash).[20] Sarah's denial of her laughter is then presented as a way for God to engage her: "The Holy One, blessed be He, never condescended to converse with a woman save with that righteous woman, and that too was through a particular cause.... And what a roundabout way He sought in order to speak with her, as it is written, *And He said, Nay, but thou didst laugh*." (MR 48.20).[21] The account of Isaac's birth is initially, and at some length, concerned with God's conversion of word to deed. Then when Isaac is named there is no mention of the significance of naming him "he will laugh": perhaps for an audience reading in Hebrew, that was simply too obvious. Instead, there is a rendering of the name as "Law" – or "a gift" – "had gone forth into the world"; and a numerological anatomization of the consonants of Isaac's name. But when Sarah utters her cry of delight, the rabbis say, "If Sarah was remembered, what did it matter to others? But when the matriarch Sarah was remembered [i.e. gave birth], many other barren women were remembered with her; many deaf gained their hearing;

DOI: 10.1057/9781137370914

many blind had their eyes opened, many insane became sane" (MR 53.9). We may note that the rabbis interpret Sarah's exultation in a purely positive light: rather than Alter's rendering, "Whoever hears will laugh *at me*," which shades from the ambiguous to the hostile, the rabbis – like Chrysostom – take Sarah's laughter as an invitation to others to laugh *with* her. Sarah's delight, just like her initial burst of disavowed laughter, is in the opinion of the rabbis performed *in public*.

It takes us outside our Judeo-Christian focus, but it is worth mentioning that Sarah laughs in the Qur'an, as well. There is something very persistent about this laughter. Although Sarah is not named, although the laughter now anticipates the news of Isaac's birth rather than responding to it, although the sense of Isaac as "laughter" is lost in the Arabic,[22] and although Isaac himself is no longer the uniquely privileged son and heir but must assume equal status with Ishmael (indeed, it is Ishmael, not Isaac, who helps his father Abraham to build the mosque at Mecca): still, Sarah laughs. Here is the Qur'an's version of the encounter at Mamre, in the new translation by Abdel Haleem:

> To Abraham Our messengers brought good news. They said, "Peace." He answered, "Peace," and without delay he brought in a roasted calf. When he saw that their hands did not reach towards the meal, he found this strange and became afraid of them. But they said, "Do not be afraid. We have been sent against the people of Lot."[23] *His wife was standing [nearby] and laughed.* We gave her good news of Isaac and, after him, of Jacob. She said, "Alas for me! How am I to bear a child when I am an old woman, and my husband here is an old man? That would be a strange thing!" They said, "Are you astonished at what God ordains? The grace of God and His blessing be upon you, people of this house! For He is worthy of all praise and glory."[24]

Sarah's laughter seems here to float in the text, unjustified and uncontextualized. Yet the earliest Islamic commentators are at pains to weave it back into its context with the sort of sympathetic engagement we have seen in Chrysostom, or the attention to her body that we have seen in Midrash. The ninth-century commentator Tabari lists no fewer than seven possible interpretations of Sarah's laughter, quoting earlier interpretations, both attributed and unattributed.[25] They range from a laugh of awe and wonder – whether at the strangers' failure to eat or at the impending destruction of the people of Lot – to a laugh engendered by Abraham's fear (this seems to be an anxious and fearful laugh: the text simply says "she laughed when she saw that Abraham was afraid") or by her own release from fear at the strangers' reassurances. One

DOI: 10.1057/9781137370914

interpretation takes the laughter out of its apparent sequence in the text of the Qur'an and returns us to something closer to the account in the Hebrew scriptures: "she laughed in wonder when she was told of Isaac, for how could it be that she would have a son in her old age and the old age of her husband?" Finally – discussed and attested at far more length than any other interpretation – there is the possibility that "she laughed" means "she began to menstruate."[26]

Tabari's own preference is for "the second interpretation, which is the report of Qatada. That is, that her laughter is the accepted sort of laughter and that it is because of her [pious] amazement about the heedlessness of the People of Lot and about God's punishment that encircled them." But the most remarkable thing about the interpretations is their breadth. Psychologically, they range from awe to anxiety to relief; the "menstruation" interpretation recognizes the corporeal miracle that is about to take place (for Sarah is ninety in the Qur'an's account as well) as well as the property we have already remarked: something overflowing, exuberant, unbounded about the nature of this laughter.

What we have seen so far is the capaciousness of laughter. Three brief descriptions of laughter (consolidated into one in the Qur'an) engender a host of interpretations. Some are committed to "hearing" the laugh, others not so; some accept, even emphasize, how rooted in the body laughter is, others turn away from the body to consider the psychology of the one who laughs. Clearly, laughter – and still more, the freighted matriarchal laughter of Sarah – is complexly expressive. It resists simple paraphrase or univocal interpretation.

The biblical account clearly portrays the laughter of both Abraham and Sarah, at the moment of the initial announcement of the birth of Isaac, as ambivalent: joyous, but doubtful.[27] On my first reading of the patristic commentaries, I thought I was going to extract a somewhat banal point about the gender bias of the church fathers: despite the similar biblical descriptions, Abraham's laughter is affirmed, while Sarah's is castigated as doubting and faithless. That would in itself, if in a limited way, have demonstrated the capaciousness of laughter, its ability to embrace different interpretative stances. But there is a richer capaciousness here. Even in these repeated attempts to fix its meaning, the laughter eludes its commentators. Its lability has little to do with the gender of the people portrayed as laughing or the gender of the commentators: it is in the nature of laughter itself. Only by acknowledging this capaciousness of laughter can we countenance the notion that laughter might be both disbelieving

DOI: 10.1057/9781137370914

and prophetic, both embarrassingly open and modestly serious, both doubtful and celebratory. Our earlier examples from Ambrose and Augustine, in particular, show those dignified thinkers struggling with this "both-and"ness, expressing the essential variety of laughter in spite of themselves. For Augustine especially, in the vast teleological design of the *City of God*, this is disconcerting: we shall see in the next chapter how he and others attempt to wrestle the capaciousness of Sarah's laughter into something more unitary and focused.

# Notes

1   The full story runs (with digressions) from Genesis 12:1 to 25:11.
2   Consider Auerbach's justly famous account of Old Testament style in his reading of the Akedah, the binding of Isaac, in the first chapter of *Mimesis*, "Odysseus' scar": its characteristics include "certain parts brought into high relief, others left obscure, abruptness, suggestive influence of the unexpressed,...development of the concept of the historically becoming, and pre-occupation with the problematic." Auerbach, E. *Mimesis: The Representation of Reality in Western Literature* tr. W. Trask (1953), new intro. E. Said (Princeton, NJ: Princeton University Press, 2003; first published in German, 1946), 23.
3   As Alter explains, the preposition *li* here is ambiguous: it may mean "'to' or 'for' or 'with' or 'at me'": *Genesis*, tr. and comm. R. Alter (New York and London: Norton, 1996), 97. The eleventh-century commentator Rashi has the joyous "whoever hears will laugh for me." Alter chooses "at"; I use "with," which is closer to the Latin and Greek renditions of late antiquity. (The King James Bible renders: "God hath made me to laugh, so that all that hear will laugh with me.") But the darker undercurrent of meaning should be borne in mind.
4   Havrelock, R. "The Myth of Birthing the Hero: Heroic Barrenness in the Hebrew Bible," *Biblical Interpretation* 16 (2008), 154–78; Baskin, J. R. *Midrashic Women: Formations of the Feminine in Rabbinic Literature* (Hanover, NH, and London: Brandeis University Press, 2002), 119–40; and especially Katz, C. E. *Levinas, Judaism, and the Feminine: the Silent Footsteps of Rebecca* (Bloomington, IN: Indiana University Press, 2003) 146–9, building on Zornberg, A. G. *The Beginning of Desire: Reflections on Genesis* (New York: Image/Doubleday, 1995). Havrelock is eloquent on the recurrent motif of near-impossibility in these births.
5   For a survey of key texts, see the final chapter of Stephen Halliwell's recent book *Greek Laughter: a Study in Cultural Psychology from Homer to Early*

DOI: 10.1057/9781137370914

*Christianity* (Cambridge: Cambridge University Press, 2008), which bears the telling title "Laughter denied, laughter deferred: the antigelastic tendencies of early Christianity"; see also Abécassis, A. "Le rire des patriarches", *Lumière et vie* 230 (December 1996), 7–14; Baconsky, T. *Le rire des Pères. Essai sur le rire dans la patristique grecque* (Paris: Desclée de Brouwer, 1996); and the essays in Mazzucco, C. (ed.) *Riso e comicità nel cristianesimo antico* (Alexandria: Edizioni dell'orso, 2007).

6 See e.g. Sarrazin, B. "Jésus n'a jamais ri. Histoire d'un lieu commun," *Recherches de science religieuse* 82 (1994), 217–22.

7 Matthew 27:41–3 and Mark 15:31 (the mockery of the priests and pharisees is omitted from Luke, though he reports the mockery of "the rulers").

8 The link between the insistence that Jesus never laughed and fear of association with Gnosticism is my own, based on the observations in Stroumsa, G. G. "Christ's Laughter: Docetic Origins Reconsidered", *Journal of Early Christian Studies* 12 (2004), 267–88; on the laughter of the Gnostics, see Gilhus, Ingvild Sælid, *Laughing Gods, Weeping Virgins: Laughter in the History of Religion* (London / New York: Routledge, 1997), 69–77.

9 Basil of Caesarea, *Regulae Fusius Tractatae*, PG 31, col. 961. In his shorter rules, he is less generous to laughter: "it is clear that it is *never* the right time (*kairos*) for laughter for a faithful person." Basil of Caesarea, *Regulae Brevius Tractatae*, PG 31, cols. 1103–4. See chapter 7 below for *kairos* and laughter.

10 For now, note that Basil illustrates his own point about *homōnymia* by citing the beatitudes on both sides of the laughter equation.

11 See Halliwell, *Greek Laughter* 515 for Basil's use of this word – not to be confused with the *hilaritas* thought desirable for the medieval monk: see Le Goff, J. "Le rire dans les règles monastiques du haut Moyen Âge", in idem, *Haut Moyen Âge: Culture, Éducation et Société* (La Garenne-Colombes 1990), 93–103; English version in Bremmer, J. and H. Roodenberg (ed.) *A Cultural History of Humour from Antiquity to the Present Day* (Cambridge, UK: Polity Press, 1997).

12 *Discant mulieres exemplis patriarcharum, discant, inquam, mulieres sequi viros suos: Hom. in Gen. 4.4.*

13 Gregory of Nazianzus, *Poemata historica: epitaphion 68*, PG 38, col. 46; see also *epitaphion* 90 (PG 38, col. 56).

14 Note, by comparison, that in his *Hebrew Questions on Genesis*, Jerome explicitly considers and then rejects the notion that Isaac takes his name from Sarah's laughter: "Isaac means laughter. Some say that he was called laughter because Sarah laughed, *which is false.* Others, because Abraham laughed – and this we approve" (Jerome, *Hebraicae Quaestiones in libro Geneseos*, ed. de Lagarde, CCL 72 (Turnhout 1959), 17.19; my emphasis).

DOI: 10.1057/9781137370914

15  For a lucid contemporary reading of *On Abraham,* see Colish, M. *Ambrose's Patriarchs: Ethics for the Common Man* (Notre Dame, IN: University of Notre Dame Press, 2005) .

16  Not having Hebrew, I read Midrash in the English translation of Rabbi Freedman. There is a wonderful modern reading of Sarah's story with its midrashic interpretations in the light of Levinasian ethics, in Chalier, C. *Les Matriarches. Sarah, Rébecca, Rachel et Léa* (Paris: Éditions du Cerf, 1985). She too wonders why the tradition treats the initial laughs of Abraham and Sarah so differently, concluding that "it might be more reassuring to separate...belief and disbelief than to appreciate their union in laughter" (47).

17  Katz remarks that Sarah's laughter both "*is* and is about eros": *Levinas, Judaism, and the Feminine*, 146.

18  *non habet in Hebraeo: Hebr. Qu. in Gen.* 21.9.

19  Alter *Genesis* ad locc.; Brenner, A. "On the semantic field of humour, laughter and the comic in the Old Testament", in Radday, Y. T., and Brenner, A. (ed.) *On Humour and the Comic in the Hebrew Bible* Bible and Literature Series 23 (Sheffield: Almond Press, 1990), 39-58. Midrash (followed, for example, by the renowned eleventh-century commentator Rashi) is particularly harsh on this last sense of "laughing," glossing it as referring to sexual immorality, idolatry, or even murder.

20  Rashi suggests that Sarah laughs "at her insides" – at the notion that her womb could produce a child.

21  This claim actually leads the rabbis into complicated straits when it comes to Hagar – with whom the bible also clearly shows God conversing.

22  I am informed that although the Arabic and Hebrew verbs "to laugh" are cognate, the sense of the name "Isaac" itself, due to a shift in pronunciation, is divorced from laughter.

23  The episode of the destruction of Sodom and Gomorrah, and the saving of Lot's family – bar his wife – is interposed, in the Hebrew scriptures, between the announcement of Isaac's birth and Sarah's delight at its accomplishment, which adds a further dark context to her laughter; here the two episodes are more tightly interwoven, though Midrash also associates the angels who destroy Sodom and Gomorrah with those who come to Abraham at Mamre: *Midrash Rabbah: Genesis* tr. H. Freedman, 2 vols. (Oxford 1939), 50.1 and 2.

24  Hud 11:69–74; see Tamer, G. "The Qur'an and Humor," in Tamer (ed.), *Humor in der arabischen Kultur* (Berlin: De Gruyter, 2009), 13. On the delicate question of whether God can be said to laugh, and on laughter and Islamic theology more generally, see Holtzman, L. " 'Does God Really Laugh?' – Appropriate and Inappropriate Descriptions of God in Islamic Traditionalist Theology," in A. Classen (ed.), *Laughter in the Middle Ages and Early Modern*

DOI: 10.1057/9781137370914

*Times: Epistemology of a Fundamental Human Behavior, its Meaning, and Consequences* (Berlin/New York: De Gruyter, 2010), 165–200.

25   I am indebted to Matthew Keegan, both for telling me about this source, and for translating it from the Arabic for me. A brief but more readily available summary of later exegesis of Sarah may be found in Stowasser, B. *Women in the Qur'an, Traditions, and Interpretation* (New York: Oxford University Press, 1994) 45–6.

26   In Midrash, when Sarah asks "Shall I have pleasure (*'ednah*)...," this is construed as a reference to menstruation (Gen. 18:12; MR 48.17). The menstruation is thus considered doubtful, in contrast to the affirmative reading in Qur'anic exegesis.

27   Their responses are different in detail, but both focus on their age, though Sarah is more explicit about their physical limitations: see Marmesh, "Anti-Covenant," in Bal, M. (ed.) *Anti-convenant. Counter-reading women's lives in the Hebrew Bible* Journal for the Study of the Old Testament Supplement Series 81 (Sheffield, England: Almond Press, 1989), 54–6.

DOI: 10.1057/9781137370914

# 2
# Sarah, Philo, and the Laugh beyond Laughter

Abstract: *This chapter stays with exegesis of Sarah's laughter, but now looks beyond interpretations* ad litteram *to explore those that interpret the episode allegorically. The first-century Hellenized Jew, Philo, plays a particularly important role in this discussion. He adverts several times to the laughter of both Abraham and Sarah, but the more philosophical importance he attaches to it, the less we can "hear" the laughter: it becomes disembodied and merely symbolic. This disembodiment of laughter passes over into Christian authors, who read it teleologically, as pointing toward the end times and the laughter of heaven.*

Conybeare, Catherine. *The Laughter of Sarah: Biblical Exegesis, Feminist Theory, and the Concept of Delight.* New York: Palgrave Macmillan, 2013. DOI: 10.1057/9781137370914.

DOI: 10.1057/9781137370914

My first chapter has given a sense of the range of late antique and early medieval commentaries on the laughter of Sarah. We have attended to the different literal, circumstantial explanations for the laughter, and we have seen how Sarah's laughter is associated with various bodily effusions – with the milk of lactation, with the blood of menstruation. But there is a vast arena of early interpretation which I have so far left untouched; and its conceptual framework persists to this day.

In chapter 1, I quoted Bishop Ambrose of Milan, providing a rather generous interpretation in the late fourth century of Sarah's first burst of laughter: "Think of this as an indication, not of disbelief, but of what was to come. For she laughed, although she still didn't know why she was laughing, because she was going to give birth to public delight in (the form of) Isaac. So she denied that she had laughed, because she didn't know; but she laughed, because she was foretelling it" (*Ab.* 1.5.43). This interpretation makes Sarah's first burst of laughter a true foretaste of the second: it is a laugh of delight, although she is ignorant of what might be causing the delight. But Sarah's second, fuller, expression of laughter is curiously under-narrated: Ambrose emphasizes the phrase "whoever hears will rejoice with me," and this, he says, refers to the generation "in which every sinner who does penance, when he is redeemed from death, displays joy [*laetitiam*] to the angels" (*Ab.* 1.7.62). That is, the reading becomes both radically generalized and entirely eschatological: it is no longer about laughter in the moment, but about the heavenly delight of the saved. (It is the more surprising that Ambrose then turns the second part of Sarah's hymn of joy into a *moralis locus* in support of breast-feeding! But I have said already that this is the view from the prosperous suburbs.)

There is a whole second part to Ambrose's treatise *On Abraham*. So far, I have quoted only from Book One. This is a book of so-called "exoteric" interpretation – scriptural interpretation for the catechumenate, those who have declared their interest in the Christian faith but have not yet been baptized. Book Two is devoted to "esoteric" interpretation, the more spiritually engaged readings for those who have now been baptized, the true initiates. Here we see fully developed the type of reading to which Sarah's "prophetic" laugh looks forward.

The principal concern of this reading is supersessionist: in other words, it erases the particularity of Abraham and Sarah's story, its ostensible location in a particular time and place of the history of the Jewish people, in favor of a Christianizing interpretation.[1] This interpretation looks to the

DOI: 10.1057/9781137370914

Christian end times and emphasizes the working of the spirit: indeed, it enacts the principle of "the spirit, not the letter." Every detail of the story is re-read in the light of Christian revelation. For example, when Abraham questions God's gift of land (Gen. 15:8), Ambrose explains, "he wanted the offspring of the church, he sought a succession that would not be servile, but free, not according to the flesh, but according to grace." Needless to say, "the church" is now identified with Sarah, the "servile succession" with the offspring of Hagar, who is equated with the synagogue. *Sara virtus vera est, vera sapientia, Agar autem est versutia tamquam ancilla perfectioris virtutis*: "Sarah is the true virtue, the true wisdom, while Hagar is the cleverness that is like a handmaid of more complete virtue." Sarah has become the *sapientia spiritalis*, spiritual wisdom, Hagar the *sapientia huius mundi*, the wisdom of this world. Moreover, when Sarah suggests that Abraham conceive a child with Hagar because she herself is barren (Gen. 16:2) it is, according to Ambrose, merely because she was waiting for the appointed time (*certo tempore*) to give birth (*Ab.* 2.10.72–4). Sarah the spiritual being, the image of the church, continues to have the gift of prophecy.

What is interesting, for my purposes, about the spiritualizing reading of Ambrose is that Sarah's laughter vanishes altogether. Abraham is allegorized as *mens*, "mind," and his laughter remains: "What does it mean when it says, 'Abraham fell on his face and laughed'? This signifies reverence: he was afraid to harm God with – as it were – free laughter [*velut libero risu*], although his laughter declared the joy of the just man, who rejoiced in such promises" (*Ab.* 2.11.86). Sarah has her roles: as church, as wisdom, and as *archousa*, the Greek word for "the one who reigns" (we shall shortly hear more of this interpretation). In her spiritual roles, she presides over the transformation from corruptible to incorruptible, from *visibilia* to *invisibilia*; in short, from the old to the new covenant, from the circumcision of the flesh to the circumcision of the heart. For this is required *ille perfectae partus iucunditatis, cuius nomen Isaac*, "that offspring of perfect delight, whose name is Isaac" – note the ambiguity of "whose": does it refer to the offspring, or the delight? But that is all we hear, in Ambrose' esoteric interpretation, of Sarah's laughter.

Origen, as I mentioned earlier, simply ignores Sarah's laughter. Twice, in fact: for he begins his homily on the birth and weaning of Isaac (*Homilies on Genesis* 7) immediately *after* Sarah's exuberant laughter at Isaac's birth. Abraham celebrates the day of Isaac's weaning with a feast, and asks,

DOI: 10.1057/9781137370914

What? Do we think it's the purpose of Holy Scripture to write stories, and tell how the boy was weaned and a feast held, how he played and did other childish things? Or should we think that scripture means to teach us something divine, and worthy for the human race to learn from the utterances (*vocibus*) of God?

Then Origen points his readers back to Paul, and Paul's distinction between Ishmael, born "of the flesh," and Isaac, born "of the spirit." He is determined not to hear Sarah's laughter, or to treat Isaac as her fleshly, embodied son.

Ambrose is not, as it were, working alone. His interpretation of Sarah and Hagar becomes the dominant one in medieval Christianity; but even in the fourth century, it is already drawing upon an interpretative tradition. Ambrose's direct antecedent is the second-century interpreter Clement of Alexandria. In Clement's compendious *Stromata*, he argues that the relationship between Sarah and Hagar shows the relationship between true, divine wisdom (*hē theia pronoia*) and worldly philosophy (*hē kosmikē paideia*, elsewhere *philosophia*). Remember Ambrose's contrast between spiritual wisdom and the wisdom of this world – "Wisdom is mistress (*kuria*) of philosophy," as Sarah was mistress of Hagar; "for philosophy is the use (*epitēdeusis*) of wisdom, while wisdom is knowledge of divine and human things" (*Strom.* 1.5). There is certainly no room for laughter here.

Clement does recognize the meaning of the name "Isaac" in another great work, the *Paedagogus*: "Isaac means laughter," *gelōs hermēneuetai ho Isaak*. However, Clement quickly distances this interpretation from any corporeal meaning:

> The king... saw Isaac playing with Rebecca, his wife and helper. The king, whose name was Abimelech, seems to me to be a sort of supramundane wisdom, looking down on the mystery of the game. The name Rebecca means "constancy." O wise game! Laughter helped by constancy, with the king looking on. The spirit of the children in Christ who live in constancy rejoices [*agalliatai*]: this is the divine game. (*Paed.* 1.5.21.3–4)

Clement here is explicitly following Philo, of whom we shall shortly hear more, and Philo insists on the importance of Isaac meaning "laughter." But there is nothing corporeal about this laughter. We cannot hear it. Consider the lack of commentary on the first line, "The king saw Isaac playing with Rebecca"; for there is no hint here that, in the biblical Hebrew, "playing" is the same word as that used for "laughing" – and has sexual overtones.[2]

DOI: 10.1057/9781137370914

The whole passage, in fact, is written under the sign of the "supramundane," the *huperkosmios*. You will remember from chapter 1 that *agalliasis* is the word specifically used for spiritual joy; its cognate verb is the one chosen to express the "divine game." The mystery, the divinity, the rejoicing spirit: all of these, constantly reiterated (for the interpretation continues in this vein), attenuate and muffle the laughter and its playfulness. The passage is so abstracted from earthly experience and from its originating narrative in the Hebrew scriptures that when Clement asserts matter-of-factly that the king's name was Abimelech, re-grounding us in the narrative, it comes as rather a surprise. Otherwise, that brief moment of "play" between Isaac and his wife immediately fades from an earthly context, and for the rest of the passage it is clear that the "divine game" is played elsewhere.

Behind at least some of this interpretation, as I have mentioned, lies Philo Judaeus, the first-century Jew who wrote in Greek and whose work seems as a result repeatedly to fall between Jewish and Christian desiderata for authority. After Clement, when he is used, it tends to be silently, in occlusion, and – as with Ambrose and his supersessionist reading of Hagar and Sarah – to ends of which he could not have approved.

And yet, for an investigation of laughter, Philo proves to be exceptionally important. For it is he who takes seriously the fact that Isaac's name means "laughter"; and he builds an entire interpretative system upon that fact. He is – so far as I have found – the only interpreter who points out that, if Isaac means "laughter," then when God asks Abraham to sacrifice Isaac what is being required is that he should sacrifice laughter.[3]

Philo glosses the episode in his *De Abrahamo*: the wise man (Philo identifies Abraham with *nous*, the intellectual part of the mind) has to sacrifice joy *dia sumbolou*, symbolically – because joy is only in its place with God. But then, if the soul has truly accepted this sacrifice, God will return the gift of joy (*Ab.* 202–3).

Philo adverts to the motif of Isaac as laughter in a number of his treatises. In *De Praemiis et Poenis*, for example, Isaac is explained as "the visible sign of invisible, spiritual joy" (31). But the heart of Philo's interpretation comes in the *De Mutatione Nominum*. When God says to Abraham (Gen. 17:16) "I shall give you a child," Philo observes that one can only truly give what is one's own – and hence, that Isaac is not a man "but the synonym [*sunōnumos*] of the best of the good sensations [*eupatheiōn*] – joy, laughter ..." (*mut. nom.* 132). Isaac is in fact, according to Philo, the son not of Abraham but of God – and Sarah's cry, "The Lord

DOI: 10.1057/9781137370914

has made laughter for me" (*mut. nom.* 137), recognizes that it was God who sowed the seed: "He made, shaped, engendered Isaac, since *he was the same as laughter* [*epeidē gelōti ho autos ēn*]." How then, asks Philo, could there have been laughter before the birth of Isaac (*mut. nom.* 157)? The soul rejoices in advance of an anticipated – a hoped-for – good; in some way, it "rejoices before joy" (*chairein pro charas*). And the day "laughs in advance," *progelai* (*mut. nom.* 161–2). Just as fear is a pain before pain, so hope is a joy before joy; and so it was natural for Abraham and Sarah to laugh, even before laughter was sown.

The laughter has become purely anticipatory – we can easily see how Ambrose reads it as "prophetic." It is the shadow of a laugh that is to come, a quasi-Platonic imitation of the real laugh that is embodied by Isaac.

At this point, Philo indulges in a short diversion, explaining the impossibility of true joy for the wicked: their joy is "pseudonymous," contrasting with the notion of Isaac as "synonymous" with laughter. He then reads the story of the birth of laughter all over again, with a somewhat different flavour. When God prophesies the birth of a child to Abraham, Abraham believes God, but not the possibility of a future child – so he responds with a wish for the child he already has, Ishmael (which means, says Philo, "listening to God," *akoē theou*): "Would that Ishmael might live in your favor!"[4] And this, Philo explains, was a reasonable response, "if Abraham could not in some way *be pregnant with Isaac*" (*mut. nom.* 252).

The choice of verb is startling, to say the least: it is *kuophorēsai*, which means "to carry a baby." The verb is occasionally used metaphorically, for example of thought (*dianoia*) bearing spiritual children – Philo himself uses it in this sense[5] – but it occurs most often in the medical corpus, in its literal sense. This makes it particularly notable that the verb should be applied to a man, for it carries the physical conditions of a woman's body along with it. Indeed, the modern commentators on Philo remark on the strangeness of the usage, and Arnaldez observes, "Applied to Abraham, the expression is undoubtedly bold, and Philo was aware of that, because he adds *pō* [in some way]."[6]

Ultimately, however, this is the moment in the text at which a more literal interpretation is superseded by an allegorical one, and the passage is glossed as follows: "So, virtue [i.e. Sarah] will bear (*texetai*[7]) a noble son for you, a male, *removed from all female emotion*, and you will name the son for the emotion which you feel in him/for him (*ep'autōi*), and you will feel completely joy (*charan*); so that you will give as name its [i.e. joy's] symbol, laughter" (*mut. nom.* 261). God's promise that Sarah will give birth in *tōi eniautōi tōi heterōi*, literally "in another year," now means not "next year," but the year which is completely other – eternity.

So now the laughter has become purely allegorical; and the shift occurred at the insertion of the audacious verb *kuophorēsai*. Laughter is borne by a man; it is "removed from all female emotion"; and its only force is eschatological. This laughter looks ahead to eternity.

Ambrose in fact expresses this notion of allegorical childbirth even more strongly. "What is holier than a mind that produces seeds of good thoughts, with which it opens the womb of the soul that has been closed off in sterility of childbearing [*pariendi*], in order that it may bring forth those generations that are invisible, that is, from that spiritual womb...?" (*Abr.* 2.11.78). This of course is a time-honored discursive strategy, dating at least from the motif of Socrates as midwife:[8] to bring the female-specific role of producing children into the spiritual, ideal, or intellectual sphere (or all three, as in Ambrose), to translate the results into the invisible realm, and generally to move from there to exclude women qua women, fleshly childbearing women, from the results.[9] But what does it mean to do this in the context of laughter – and specifically, in the context of Sarah's laughter?

Even Philo, who places laughter at the centre of his cosmology, who prays that the whole of creation should be raised up by God and laugh (*mut. nom.* 156), cannot hear the laughter of the woman at the heart of this story. In making Isaac truly *be* laughter, in fact, he occludes the laughter that accompanied his moment of birth. Once we have the paradoxical identification of laughter with a human being, then we move into the symbolic realm: what does it really mean to say that laughter is the symbol of the joy that Abraham felt at Isaac's birth (*mut. nom.* 261)? Ironically, when laughter somehow *becomes* a body, as in Philo, it is no longer situated *in* the body.

And moreover – still following Philo – this laughter has nothing to do with Sarah. This miraculous son, born of virtue and mind (*aretē* and *nous* – Sarah and Abraham) is guaranteed to be "removed from all female emotion." Of course he is. He is reaching forward, out of the timebound world of childbirth and laughter, into the disembodied world of invisible, transcendent properties. As soon as we hear the claim that a man can *kuophorēsai*, bear a child, we know that we have moved into the realm

DOI: 10.1057/9781137370914

of the symbolic, and we can no longer hear the laughter. In fact, Sarah's distinctive laughter of delight is no longer there to be heard.

Once laughter has evaporated in transcendence, can it still be laughter? Ecclesiastes reads, "To everything there is a season, and a time to every purpose under the heaven... A time to weep, and a time to laugh" (Eccl. 3:1 and 4). But the reading of laughter that Christian interpreters built upon Philo deferred that laughter to the end times. The beatitudes play a crucial role in this: "Blessed are you who weep now; you will laugh for joy... Woe upon you who laugh now; you shall mourn and weep" (Luke 6:21, 25). There is no longer a purpose for laughter "under the heaven." The only appropriate "time to laugh" was in the eschatological moment, the time of salvation after death. By the later middle ages, heaven can be referred to simply as the "land of laughter."[10]

This is especially important for Christian readings of Sarah. When commentators refuse to hear her laughter, refuse to see it as situated in a miraculous embodied moment, and defer it to the end times, then it makes possible too a wholesale, ongoing deferral or erasure of Jewish truth in favor of Christian revelation. Hence the attempt, alluding to which I concluded chapter 1, to "wrestle the capaciousness of Sarah's laughter into something more unitary and focussed."

Augustine's reading of Sarah's laughter, in his great work of Christian teleology *The City of God*, is a case in point. For him, Sarah is the "type" – the foreshadowing, representative figure – of the New Testament, Hagar the type of the Old. In turn, they respectively represent spiritual, intellective interpretation, and bodily interpretation. The New Testament, like Sarah, is "free," the Old, like Hagar, "enslaved" – subordinated, that is, to Christian, supersessionist interpretation (*civ.* 13.21).

Augustine subsequently re-reads the whole narrative of Abraham and Sarah under the sign of grace. In Genesis 17, Isaac is "the son of the promise,"

> by whom grace, not nature, is signified, because a son is promised from an old man and a barren old woman. For although God may also effect the natural outcome of procreation, yet where nature is vitiated and breaks down, the work of God is clear, and grace is understood even more clearly. (*civ.* 16.26)

Because – writes Augustine – this will happen "not through birth, but through rebirth," it is at this point in the biblical narrative that God commands Abraham to be circumcised – and not just Abraham, but his

DOI: 10.1057/9781137370914

servants and household, because circumcision, which represents grace, is promised to all.

> For what does circumcision signify, if not nature renewed with old age sloughed off?...Even the names of the parents are changed; everything resonates with newness, and the new testament is foreshadowed in the old. (*civ*. 16.26)

And here is where Abraham laughs his laughter, "the exultation of the joyful, not the derision of the faithless" – who now look like the obdurate Jews who will not accept that "the new testament is foreshadowed in the old." When Isaac is born, indeed, and both his father and his mother have laughed, Hagar is thrown out of the house – and the expulsion of Hagar is read as the expulsion of the old covenant, displaced by Sarah, the new one; "whence Sarah bears the *figura* of the heavenly Jerusalem, that is, the city of God" (*civ*. 16.31).

Grace is the mechanism of supersession: of Sarah's displacement of Hagar, of the new testament's displacement of the old. And the mark of supersession is circumcision – but circumcision of the heart, not of the foreskin, as Paul had taught in the earliest texts of Christian scripture:

> For he is not a Jew, which is one outwardly; neither is that circumcision, which is but outward in the flesh: but he is a Jew, which is one inwardly; and circumcision is that of the heart, in the spirit, and not in the letter; whose praise is not of men, but of God. (Rom. 2:28–9)

Deuteronomy – that is, a key book of the Hebrew scriptures – talks of circumcision of the heart, too (Deut. 10:16[11] and 30:6), but not in the context of erasing corporeal, "literal," circumcision. And when the rabbis respond to the covenant of circumcision made by God with Abraham, they expressly consider, and reject, other possible interpretations:

> Nakdah said: It is written, *And he that is eight days old shall be circumcised among you, every male* (Gn. 17:12). Now if he is circumcised at the ear, he cannot hear; at the mouth, he cannot speak; *at the heart, he cannot think.* Where then could he be circumcised and yet be able to think? Only at the *'orlah* of the body [i.e. the foreskin]. Rabbi Tanhuma observed: this argument of Nakdah is logical. (MR 46.5; my emphasis)

Midrash is aware of the notion of circumcision of the heart, and refuses it in favor of literal circumcision. And no wonder. Interpreted through the circumcision of the heart, Sarah becomes a type for the new testament (and Isaac, "he-will-laugh," incidentally becomes a type for Christ).

DOI: 10.1057/9781137370914

Typology is the ultimate teleological narrative, in which everything looks toward Christ's coming and his return at Judgement. And for Christians from Paul onward, typological readings are set up by the re-inscription of Abraham's fleshly circumcision as a spiritual one. "In his new theology of circumcision," writes Kathleen Biddick, "...Paul severed a Christian 'now' from a Jewish 'then.'"[12]

I remarked in chapter 1 on the way in which Sarah's laughter resonates in the other great exultant moments of birth in the Bible. In the Hebrew scriptures, the closest parallel is the vocal delight of Hannah when she dedicates Samuel in the temple. Augustine, in the *City of God*, quotes Hannah's song of delight in full, and then observes:

> Will these be thought of as the words of one little woman [*muliercula*], rejoicing because a son has been born to her? Is the human mind turned so far away from the light of truth as not to perceive that the words she poured out surpassed the capacity of a woman [*modum feminae*]? Rather, won't the person who is fittingly moved...by these events strain towards and see and know that through this woman, whose name, Hannah, means Christ's grace,[13] is spoken in the spirit of prophecy the actual Christian religion, the actual city of God,... in short the actual grace of God...? (*civ.* 17.4)

The delight of the moment is occluded by its foreshadowing of grace, just as the body of the "one little woman" from whom the delight emerges is occluded by its abstract, disembodied significance.

My contention, therefore, is that if we strive to hear the laughter of Sarah, we are well placed to reverse the teleological tendencies of thought that have become so habitual in Christian or para-Christian interpretation, the "typological imaginary."[14] What does an inarticulable eruption of human delight have to do with typology and the end times? Sarah's laughter challenges the system of knowledge and meaning that claims its validity from a view *sub specie aeternitatis*, beneath the gaze of eternity. In the following chapters, we shall try to stop erasing the particular – the *muliercula* – in favor of the universal; we shall try to pause and attend to the corporeal instead of to the spiritual, and see what emerges.

# Notes

1    On this type of maneuver, see also Conybeare, C. "*sanctum, lector, percense uolumen*: Snakes, Readers, and the Whole Text in Prudentius' *Hamartigenia*,"

DOI: 10.1057/9781137370914

in *The Early Christian Book* ed. W. Klingshirn and L. Safran (Washington DC, 2007), with further references there.

2    As we remarked in chapter 1.

3    I do wonder, though, whether this is behind the rabbinic interpretation of the aftermath of the Akedah – that is, the binding of Isaac: that Sarah died of grief, thinking her son was dead. A similar connection is made by the early Islamic interpreters: "When Sarah learned what God wanted with Isaac, she fell ill for two days and died on the third." Al-Ṭabarī, *The History of al-Ṭabarī*, volume II: *Prophets and Patriarchs*, tr. W. Brinner (Albany: State University of New York Press, 1987), 68.

4    Gen. 17:18; Philo, *De Mutatione Nominum* ed. Arnaldez, Les Oeuvres de Philon d'Alexandrie 18 (Paris 1964), 201–2.

5    See Philo, *De Sacrificiis Abelis et Caini*, ed. Méasson, Les Oeuvres de Philon d'Alexandrie 4 (Paris 1966), 102 of the power in the soul "through which thought carries a baby (*phorei*) and has birth pains (*ōdinei*) and gives birth to (*apotiktei*) many things." My translation; the most recent translations, in both English (the Loeb) and French (*Oeuvres de Philon*) obscure the corporeality of the images.

6    "Appliquée à Abraham, l'expression est sans doute audacieuse, et Philon en a conscience puisqu'il ajoute *pō*": Arnaldez in *mut. nom.*, p. 151; my translation.

7    Not *kuophorēsei*: the problematic verb is not repeated here (where it might be more appropriate).

8    See Plato, *Theaetetus*, ed. Burnet, OCT, tr. and ann., J. McDowell (Oxford: Clarendon Press, 1973), 148e–151d, for an extended development of the metaphor of Socrates as midwife.

9    A vigorous critique of this notion: see Irigaray, L. "Sorcerer Love: A Reading of Plato, *Symposium*, 'Diotima's Speech,'" in *An Ethics of Sexual Difference* tr. C. Burke and G. Gill (London: Athlone Press, 1993), 20–33, on Diotima's speech in Plato's *Symposium* – and see further below.

10   See e.g. Archpoet, *Die Gedichte des Archipoeta* ed. Wathenphul and Krefeld (Heidelberg: C. Winter, 1958), Poem 5, where heaven is the *terra ridentium.*

11   "Circumcise therefore the foreskin of your heart, and be no more stiff-necked."

12   Biddick, K. *The Typological Imaginary: Circumcision, Typology, History* (Philadelphia: University of Pennsylvania Press, 2003), 12. This book explores the egregious, exclusionary ways in which the notion has been used through time; it attempts to analyze "supersessionary thinking" and unbind "the typological imaginary" in order "to open up encounter [between Christians and Jews] to less constrained, less deadening historiographical habits of mind."

13   The Latin is not quite so bald – *per hanc mulierem, cuius etiam nomen, id est Anna, gratia eius interpretatur* – but I think that the referent of "eius" must be Christ.

DOI: 10.1057/9781137370914

14  Biddick again: "figure and letter are both real and possible and... they
    therefore are always doubled and consequently can also be *self-reversing*.
    In other words, there is nothing to guarantee the irreversibility of figural
    thinking *except the theological notion of supersession.*" *Typological Imaginary* 6;
    her emphasis.

DOI: 10.1057/9781137370914

# 3

# Laughter and Power

*Abstract: Now we turn to major twentieth-century theorists of laughter. In this chapter, the theories of Henri Bergson and Sigmund Freud are summarized and discussed: they are grouped together under the loose notion of theorists concerned with power dynamics in laughter, between laughing people. They are particularly interested in laughter as social corrective (Bergson) or an eruption of the socially repressed (Freud). Different types of power dynamics are discussed, to conclude that these theories – for all their perspicacity – do not aptly capture the laughter of Sarah, which is only vestigially concerned with power.*

Conybeare, Catherine. *The Laughter of Sarah: Biblical Exegesis, Feminist Theory, and the Concept of Delight.* New York: Palgrave Macmillan, 2013.
DOI: 10.1057/9781137370914.

DOI: 10.1057/9781137370914

Let us go back to Sarah's cry of joy:

> "Laughter has God made me;
>> Whoever hears will laugh with me."

Laughter can exclude or include: there are few feelings more abject than being present while others laugh at something one does not understand; there are few more delightful than sharing the laughter of a group. This is one of the reasons the ambiguity of the preposition in Sarah's exclamation is so interesting: it makes all the difference whether the preposition should be understood as "with" or "at"; and yet it is simultaneously both.

The ability of laughter to include or exclude suggests a certain intersection between laughter and power; many of the copious modern writings on laughter have dwelt more or less explicitly upon this, and I shall offer my own account of their interrelation shortly.[1] In recent years, however, it has become conventional to propose a tripartite division in theories about the sources of laughter, that between superiority, incongruity, and release.[2]

The *locus classicus* for the formulation of laughter as an expression of superiority, although it builds (as Quentin Skinner has recently shown[3]) on Renaissance writing on laughter as an expression of contempt, is the description offered by Hobbes, first in the *Leviathan*, then in *Human Nature*:

> the passion of laughter is nothing else but sudden glory arising from some sudden conception of some eminency in ourselves, by comparison with the infirmity of others, or with our own formerly... (*Human Nature* 4:46)[4]

This notion of laughter as an eruption of perceived superiority gets deeply embedded in the tradition. When, at the turn of the twentieth century, Henri Bergson composes his seminal essay on laughter, he writes toward the end, "Laughter is, above all, a correction. Made to humiliate, it necessarily gives a painful impression to the person who is its object" (150).[5]

The release theory of laughter – laughter as an expression of relief after the build-up of nervous tension – was given its most extensive and thoughtful articulation by Freud, and I shall address it, and other aspects of Freud's account of laughter, later in this chapter. As for incongruity, that too is given one of its cardinal expressions by Bergson. Incongruity tends to be grounded in disproportion, absurdity, awkwardness or

DOI: 10.1057/9781137370914

grandiosity; it may express itself either corporeally – with a stumble, a protuberance, a pompous air – or in a play of words – exaggeration or malapropism, for example. But it is, above all, about what we laugh *at*, not about the dynamics of laughter; and my focus is on laughter itself, not on its causes.

The theories of both superiority and release seem to me fundamentally to be about the power relations in the situations that cause laughter; these leave largely out of account the corporeal dynamics of laughter, the way in which being in the body is basic to laughter and the laughing subject. And so I find more expressive a simple division between theories of laughter that engage power dynamics – whether (as more commonly) from the dominant side, or from the subordinate – and those that are grounded in the relationship between laughter and the body. The division between the two is not impermeable, as we shall see; but it is a useful delineation of emphasis. The first group of theories I shall explore in this chapter, with a reading of Bergson and Freud; the theories that put embodied experience in the foreground I shall explore in the next. In each case, my reading is attuned particularly to whether they can account for the laughter of delight.

Notwithstanding the title of his essay, *Le Rire*, Bergson is preoccupied with the causes and purposes of laughter, not with laughter itself. His first example of what causes laughter is when someone trips and falls. "The passers-by laugh" (7), which they wouldn't if their unfortunate source of merriment had simply sat down voluntarily. From here Bergson comes naturally to his famed formulation of the cause of laughter as a perception *du mécanique plaqué sur du vivant*, "of the mechanical encrusted upon the living" (29). What prompts laughter are the moments when, as it were, the strings of the human puppet are disclosed; when the basis of the "natural" is called into question by a moment of apparent artificality. *Au fond*, we are reminded that it is a clumsy fallible body that clothes the living soul; and we laugh. But we should note, although Bergson does not, that the clumsy body necessarily belongs to someone else. We are not, in his account, laughing at our own stumblings. Bergson insists that a key ingredient of the conditions for laughter is the *insociabilité* of the person involved (111) – the way in which they are not properly embedded in social networks.[6] There will always be a sense of dislocation between the person and their surroundings, whether the surroundings are their social interactions or the pitfalls of the physical world. The person doing the

DOI: 10.1057/9781137370914

laughing will always be someone other than the object of laughter; and this laughter requires "a fleeting anaesthesia of the heart" (*une anesthésie momentanée du coeur*, 4), for it is, writes Bergson, purely to do with intellect and disengaged from emotion. Hence, the *insensibilité* of the spectator will be the counterpart of the *insociabilité* of the unfortunate who trips and falls. The imagined scenario for laughter is always oppositional: there is always a party who will be humiliated and corrected in some way. The dynamic, as in Hobbes, is of a lebel laugher vaunting his superiority over a victim. Laughter, for Bergson, is an act of social aggression.

Bergson is important because his essay is a cardinal point in the history of writing about laughter. Versions of his opposition between the *mécanique* and the *vivant* crop up in almost every subsequent formulation of the dynamics of laughter, albeit under other names. The grounding dualism of the *mécanique* and the *vivant* accompanies another equally pervasive dualism, of the intellect and the emotions. As I have said, Bergson insists on dissevering laughter from emotion, and claiming that it is all about an intellectual response.[7]

There are hints of something very different in Bergson's account, however. For all his insistence that laughter is divorced from emotion, he talks about childhood games in a way that links the two. "Too often, we speak of our feelings of pleasure and pain as if they were born fullgrown, as if each one did not have its own history" (51).[8] Out of childhood games, and a childhood sense of the comical, comes the laughter of the adult: a "feeling of pleasure" does not emerge only out of the disengaged intellectualism of the moment, but out of a complex relationship with the memory of former pleasures, games, and delights. Emotion keeps bubbling up; it cannot quite be contained.

Bergson goes on to distinguish between the witty – *spirituel*, relating to *l'esprit* – and the comic (79); the witty relates specifically to words, and is played out *sub specie theatri* (Bergson's formulation, 81). His starting point is an expression from Mme. de Sévigné, writing to sympathize with her daughter's illness: "J'ai mal à votre poitrine," "I'm ill in your chest" – or "your chest hurts me." A play on words, yes, but one that is empty without the introduction of emotional sympathy. The witty, at least, may relate to the emotions – though that's not an aspect on which Bergson comments explicitly – perhaps precisely because of the theatrical element: we are being invited to visualize a scenario more fully. Ultimately, he writes, "language only attains laughable results because it is a human product,

DOI: 10.1057/9781137370914

modelled as exactly as possible on the forms of the human mind (*l'esprit humain*)" (99).

Perhaps it is a certain pessimism about *l'esprit humain* that leads Bergson to the anomalous final page or so of his book. Having pursued his exploration of the comic in a largely passionless key, he observes that in the laugher, "we speedily discern a degree of egoism and, behind this, something less spontaneous and more bitter" (152). Society, writes Bergson, is like the sea: stable in the depths, while its waves are forever at odds with each other on the surface and tipped with the foam of laughter. A child at play may pick up a handful of the sea-foam, and be astonished to be left with only a little salty residue.

> Laughter arises just like that foam. It marks superficial revolts on the sur-
> face of social life. ... Like froth, it fizzes; it is gaiety. But the philosopher who
> picks it up to taste a little will sometimes find a certain amount of bitterness
> in place of a tiny bit of matter. (153)

The last word of the work is *amertume*, bitterness. Bergson's laughter vanishes like sea-foam in a child's hands. Does laughter have something to do with the emotions after all?

Bergson strives to make laughter symptomatic of an intellectual response – but his own writing keeps pushing him in a different direction. That he ends in bitterness is revealing.[9] The emotions of laughter cannot quite be suppressed. Laughter is excessive; it spills over. We consider Sarah's laugh of delight, and it refuses the oppositions that Bergson tries to impose: it is not about the absurdity of "the mechanical encrusted upon the living," but about the joy in life itself. It is not about reason as opposed to emotion, but an outburst of delight in the face of the utterly irrational – which has in fact come to be. Above all, Sarah's laughter is not an outburst of social aggression; it is not oppositional of its very nature. There may indeed be a little bitterness: look at the ambiguity between "all who hear" laughing with and laughing at her. This merely shows the plenitude of emotions in her laughter, a plenitude which Bergson tries to control but cannot entirely erase, even from his own work. Sarah is not asserting her own power, and there is no abject recipient of her laughter.[10]

We are considering an instance of laughter, not a joke; nevertheless, Freud's contribution to the discussion cannot be ignored.[11] *The Joke and its Relation to the Unconscious* was published in 1905, only five years after Bergson's study of laughter.[12] *The Joke* traces the origin of laughter to the

DOI: 10.1057/9781137370914

release in the person laughing of psychic energy which had previously been used in repression (128) or simply – somehow – elsewhere (142): as a result, Freud's account of laughter works best for what he calls the "tendentious joke," in which a hostile or obscene impulse is diverted into a joke. (Freud was simultaneously composing "Three essays on the theory of sexuality," trying to explain sexual pleasure.) Freud had read Bergson, and cites him with approval (201 ff.); but unlike Bergson, he shows an unabashed appreciation for sources of delight removed from the constraints of the intellect. He reverts repeatedly to the image of the child at play – in the account of jokes, the child uses play "to escape the pressure of critical reason" (121); in the account of the comic, he remarks on the child's "laughter of pure pleasure" at a successful imitation, and says that the comic is the "lost laughter of childhood regained" (217). This is not unexpected: "the infantile is the source of the unconscious" (164), and Freud sees the joke as "developed play."[13] But the high value that Freud seems to place on recapturing the laughter of childhood is surprising. Is it about the reopening of connections with "the source of the unconscious"? It extends even to a rhapsodic passage on the value of alcohol for reducing inhibition: "the adult becomes a child again, finding pleasure in having the course of his thoughts freely at his disposal without having to keep to the compulsion of logic" (122). Something very important is creeping in here amid the more systematic exposition of Freud's theory: an appreciation for the inexpressible in laughter, the defiance of reason, the uncontrollability of laughter, and the connection of laughter with pleasure.[14]

My excerption of these passages is due to my own preoccupation with the laughter of delight: I find Freud's scattered tributes to unbridled joy in children and the child-like fascinating. They are ancillary to his argument in *The Joke*; but the child is, in a sense, at the heart of his much later essay "Humour" (1927). Here the super-ego is cast, in ways largely unanticipated in *The Joke*, in the role of comforting parent to the child-like ego: it "tries, by means of humour, to console the ego and protect it from suffering," saying in effect "Look! Here is the world, which seems so dangerous! It is nothing but a game for children, just worth making a jest about."[15] Clearly Freud felt that there was a version of the dynamics of laughter that he had left unexplored in the earlier text – and it hinges on the image of inviting a child to laugh.

However, dwelling on the interstitial images of the child – always seen playing in isolation – obscures the power dynamics of Freud's earlier

DOI: 10.1057/9781137370914

exposition in *The Joke*. In the case of the tendentious joke, three people are envisaged as participating: the hearer of the joke, "in whom the joke's intention of producing pleasure is fulfilled"; the speaker, whose laughter is enabled by the hearer's laughter; and the object of the joke, "who is taken as the object of the hostile or sexual aggression" (95). The first two are men, the third a woman, of whose response to the laughter we are not told. Freud reenacts this triad again and again as he tells jokes about women to his presumptively male reader; he also persistently tells jokes about Jews, implying that his reader is not just male but Christian. (*The Joke* had its origins in a collection of Jewish jokes which Freud compiled and subsequently burned.)

Sarah Kofman has done an audacious Freudian reading of Freud here, exploring the importance of the third party in making it possible for the other two to overcome their internal criticism, or repression.[16] She points to Freud's "castration" of both Jew and woman, and his simultaneous concealment of the castration "behind a universalising humanism," *derrière un humanisme universaliste*, since both are subsumed into the category of *Menschenkind*, "humankind."[17] The culmination of her reading of *The Joke* relies, fittingly for our topic, on an anecdote related by Freud of a woman in childbirth.

> The doctor who has been requested to attend the Baroness at her confinement declares that the moment has not yet arrived, and suggests to the Baron that meantime they play a game of cards in the next room. After a while the Frau Baronin's cry of pain reaches the ears of the two men: 'Ah mon Dieu, que je souffre.' The husband leaps up, but the doctor detains him: 'It's nothing. Let's carry on playing.' A while later they hear her crying out in labour: 'Mein Gott, mein Gott, was für Schmerzen!' – 'Won't you go in, Professor?' asks the Baron. 'No, no, it's still not time.' – Finally, from the next room they hear an unmistakable cry of 'Ai, waih, waih' [Oi vey]: then the doctor throws away his cards and says: 'It's time'.

The tripartite structure here is perfectly clear, as is the fact that the agonized Baroness, descending through the orders of linguistic superiority until she expresses her wretchedness in Yiddish, will take no part in the laughter. Freud tells the story twice, first as an example of a joke, then as an example of "the comic," and specifically of the technique of comic "unmasking."[18] The first time the Baroness descends into Yiddish, Freud interprets it as "the primitive," abstracting the Jewish specificity into a universal category; the second time, he reads it as a stripping away of

DOI: 10.1057/9781137370914

social class, until the Baroness is simply a basic, bodily woman (*Pourquoi* 189; 191). Never, Kofman observes, does Freud address "la spécificité juive." And yet perhaps, she suggests, as Freud brings *The Joke* to birth, he reveals himself as he cries out: he "would like to hide his castrated aspect [literally, "face"] – feminine or Jewish – behind the universal one of Man" (197).

The point, for our purposes, is twofold. First, we see – for I think Kofman's analysis is correct – the tendency to a creeping universalism which theories of laughter seem somehow to enable. In Freud's case, it comes in the implicit denial of the specificity of his subjects (and even on his own terms, without specific subjects, where is the joke?), and indeed of the specificity of his own subject position. In Bergson's case, the universalism lies in the account of the causes of laughter – in the mechanical, the repetitious, the "typical" – and in the insistence on the policing effect of "society." The tensions and inconsistencies that arise from the universalist claims in each thinker's account suggest that they are in practice unsustainable.

The second point lies in the power dynamics implicit in each account – by which I mean the specific dynamics of superiority and inferiority. In each case, the laugher is envisaged as laughing at – against – not just something, but some*one* else. Laughter is conceived as a way of asserting superiority, an act of social aggression. Bergson's case, at least on the face of it, is quite simple: laughter as "social corrective" implies the superiority of the person who knows how to act appropriately – and the exertion of the power of derision to force those out of place, voluntarily or otherwise, to conform. Freud's power dynamics are hidden in plain sight: almost every joke cited concerns the unmasking of pretension, the reduction of a subject (usually a woman or a Jew) to its purportedly true, subordinate state; but Freud does not analyze his jokes in these terms. Nor does he make explicit the power dynamics engaged by himself as narrator and framer of the jokes. In fact, he is setting himself up as the ultimate arbiter of the laugh of superiority – but only at the cost of implicitly denying who and what he is.

Let us measure this explicitly against our laughter of delight. The assertion of superiority does not begin to describe the laughter of Sarah. In neither instance does her laughter vaunt a superior position. In both cases, her laughter acknowledges the impossible and incredible – first, in anticipation, with baffled amusement; then, in fulfilment, with awed delight. The laughter exists for itself: it would come whether there were

DOI: 10.1057/9781137370914

anyone to hear it or not. If people do hear, they will join in, each in their own way – "whoever hears will laugh with me" – or at me, or for me – but it is not necessary. And her laughter certainly does not claim some sort of superiority to God: God has created the conditions for the laughter, the impossible event which happens, and God is given the credit.

But power dynamics are, of course, not only the dynamics of domination: they may also be those of submission. They may divert or disclaim power, or re-appropriate it from a subordinate position. Having said this, the laugh of submission – the reluctant laugh before the aggressor, the laugh, perhaps, of Freud's woman or Jew, the third party attempting hopelessly to join in the joke – is in general strangely inaudible: in analyses of laughter, the theoreticians have tended to side with the aggressor.

Freud, to be sure, analyzes briefly the way in which hostile jokes "bribe the listener" and substitute for action; he observes of such humor that, like caricature, "we laugh at it even when it is badly done, merely *because we consider rebellion against authority to be a creditable thing*" (100, my emphasis). Here, the scenario is of the first person (man) launching a joke against the second, eliciting the support of the ever-passive third. "We" who consider rebellion against authority creditable are still clearly men. This is, however, an important type of laughter – the laugh of subversion, the laughter which expresses defiance even in apparently hopeless circumstances.

This dynamic is differently captured, for the visual arts, by Jo Anna Isaak. She discusses the way in which feminist artists, particularly Barbara Kruger, have tried to mobilize the third feminized element of the Freudian triad: to introduce a dynamic subjectivity into the triad, instead of the mere passive recipient that Freud seems to envision. She writes of Kruger's "famous accusatory 'You,'" which is addressed to the male viewer, but then notes that "The 'We' her work addresses is any subject seeking to shift the limits of his or her enclosure – through pleasure and laughter."[19]

The laughter claimed by the Christian martyrs is an extreme example of this type: the laughter that embarrasses and discomfits the face of authority, the laughter that disdains violence and triumphs even in death.[20] The laughing martyr cannot arrest his or her own death; he can only protect against the abjection desired by his persecutors. For martyrs, such laughter can only be claimed as a victory in an economy of meaning that resists closure in the temporal world, and insists on opening out into the spiritual or metaphysical one. The language of a martyr's

DOI: 10.1057/9781137370914

laughter can only be considered to have truly subversive meaning if it reaches into the afterlife, and continues there. This, in a sense, returns us to the typological imaginary: the laughter is in some sense displaced out of the present, out of the person laughing, and onwards into a posited and abstracted future.

But subversive laughter may be complete in itself: it may get its satisfaction simply from its own existence. In this sense, it works from within repression merely to posit a context where laughter is permitted. Subversive laughter produces discomfiture because of the way in which it proposes its own language: a figure of authority cannot argue with or answer back to someone laughing. If they try to do so, they become more laughable. They can only choose whether or not to join in the laughter. We shall explore later this propensity of laughter to create its own language.

The laughter of submission seems to me hollow, produced out of an abject complaisance, in no way the irrepressible moment of delight that is our concern. But against the odds, subversive laughter may be the laughter of delight: an infectious welling up of joy even in the most unpromising circumstances. The constraints of the world are shown for an instant to be absurd: hilarity![21]

There is a third type of laughter from the underside of the power dynamic that is arguably more widespread than either of the previous two, though still less analyzed. This is the laughter of the subordinate which neither colludes with authority nor attempts to overthrow it: it is simply laughter as a coping mechanism, a way of affirming community and dealing with the quotidian injustices of life. Sully is the only theoretician of laughter whom I have noticed remarking on this: "How many men [*sic*] in one of the highly civilised communities of to-day may have learned to keep their heads above the water by the practice of a gentle laughter, no one knows..."[22] But in default of theory, we may turn to literature. Out of an abundance of literary examples of such laughter, a passage from Toni Morrison's *Song of Solomon* encapsulates it particularly well. A group of black men in a barber's shop in the Northern US try to digest the news of the death of Emmett Till in Mississippi:[23]

> The men began to trade tales of atrocities, first stories they had heard, then those they'd witnessed, and finally the things that had happened to themselves. A litany of personal humiliation, outrage, and anger turned sicklelike back to themselves as humor. They laughed then, uproariously, about the speed with which they had run, the pose they had assumed, the

DOI: 10.1057/9781137370914

ruse they had invented to escape or decrease some threat to their manliness, their humanness.[24]

This laughter used as a coping mechanism from a subordinate subject position we might call subrision, from the Latin verb *subridere*. This verb provides the etymological root of the French *sourire*, to smile; but originally it means "to laugh from beneath," whether slyly, as if from behind a hand, or simply, more generally, from a position of disadvantage. Not surprisingly, this type of laughter is particularly prevalent in African American literature: Ralph Ellison ponders a complicated instance of it in his essay "An Extravagance of Laughter," writing of the way in which comedy "allow[s] us to laugh at that which is normally *un*laughable."[25] The "us" here is the subordinate third person of the Freudian triad (though Ellison does not express it this way), who through "subrision" can begin to live and move and claim independent subjective being. Can we say that subrision expresses delight? I think not: it seems to me a response forced by circumstance, rather than bursting beyond circumstance.[26] But Ellison might disagree: I have read his essay again and again, trying to hear whether the laughter that engulfs him is the sound of delight or simply of release. Perhaps the two cannot be so clearly distinguished from each other.

Before we leave the notion of laughter from the wrong side of a power dynamic, a subordinate subject position, we should consider one more type of laughter, the laughter – difficult though it is truly to imagine – of humility. One contemporary thinker, Simon Critchley, makes the laughter of humility an important part of his notion of the ethical subject. This is, above all, the ability to laugh at oneself that we noted was absent from Bergson's project. (Paradoxically, it is vestigially present in Freud's, but only to the degree that he consents to be unmasked as Jewish.) "Humour," writes Critchley, "recalls us to the modesty and limitedness of the human condition"; this seems to suit Sarah, who is certainly aware of her "modesty and limitedness" in the face of God: "laughter has God made me." But Critchley continues, "...a limitedness that calls not for tragic-heroic affirmation but comic *acknowledgement*, not Promethean authenticity but laughable inauthenticity."[27] In the context of Critchley's own argument, this bespeaks an endearing humility, a lack of grandiosity, in an ethical subject position. But it will not work for Sarah. Her laughter is in no way about inauthenticity: it is an acknowledgement, on the contrary, of a magnificent truth. And yet at the same time it is not "tragic-heroic." It is not grandiose, and it does not make grandiose claims

DOI: 10.1057/9781137370914

about her own subject position. It is simply an unstoppable ebullition of delight. We realize why there is such a gulf between the two on realizing that Critchley builds his notion of the laughter of humility on Beckett's *risus purus*, "the laugh that laughs at the laugh, the laugh that laughs at that which is unhappy."

Sarah's laughter is not "at the laugh" or "at that which is unhappy." In its own way, it is subversive, but it is not laughing *at* anything. The peculiarity of this laughter is that it simply *is*. It exists for itself, in its moment. It expresses neither aggression nor submission. It is unique, and it requires no audience. When the laughter of children bubbles into the texts of Bergson and – more particularly – Freud, it performs its own ungovernability and irrationality; it is playing, refusing to be enclosed in neatly organized theories. Just as in life, such laughter is not susceptible to systematic notions of etiology or causation; it cannot be accounted for by affirmation or disruption of power structures. This laughter, the laughter of delight, simply is.

# Notes

1   See Parvalescu, A. *Laughter: Notes on a Passion* (Cambridge, MA: MIT Press, 2010), chapter 1, on early modern instances of laughter and control.
2   This tripartite division was proposed by Morreall, J. *Taking Laughter Seriously* (Albany NY: State University of New York Press, 1983); it is echoed by e.g. Lippitt, in his set of articles on laughter; Critchley, S. *On Humour* (London and New York: Routledge, 2002), 2–3.
3   Skinner, Q. "Hobbes and the classical theory of laughter," in idem, *Visions of Politics* vol. 3 (Cambridge: Cambridge University Press, 2002), 142–76.
4   Hobbes, T. *Human Nature*, in *The English Works of Thomas Hobbes* ed. W. Molesworth, vol. 4 London: John Bohn, 1840; first published 1640), 1–76. "Sudden glory" is constantly adverted to in writings on laughter: for contemporary examples, see e.g. Lippitt, J. "Humour and Superiority", *Cogito* 9 (1995), 54–61; Parvalescu, *Laughter*, again.
5   Bergson, H. *Le Rire: essai sur la signification du comique* (Paris: Quadrige/PUF, 1940 [first published 1900]); English translation by W. Sypher in *Comedy* (Baltimore and London: Johns Hopkins University Press, 1956), 61–190. Page numbers refer to the French edition; the translation is my own. On Bergson, see e.g. Moore, F. C. T. *Bergson: Thinking Backwards* (Cambridge: Cambridge University Press, 1996); Prusak, B. "Le rire à nouveau: Rereading Bergson," in *Journal of Aesthetics and Art Criticism* 62 (2004), 377–88.

DOI: 10.1057/9781137370914

6    Bergson's contemporary Sully also emphasizes the importance of social
     networks in his *An Essay on Laughter: its forms, its causes, its development and
     its value* (London, New York, Bombay: Longmans, Green, and co., 1902).

7    In this too, he is following established tradition: think of the eighteenth-
     century aphorism of Horace Walpole, "This world is a comedy to those that
     think, a tragedy to those that feel."

8    "Trop souvent nous parlons de nos sentiments de plaisir et de peine *comme
     s'ils naissaient vieux*, comme si chacun d'eux n'avait pas son histoire." "Comme
     s'ils naissaient vieux," "as if they were born old": a poignant formulation.

9    Compare e.g. the critique of Mary Douglas, who objects to the way in which
     Bergson imports "moral judgement" to laughter: see "Jokes," in eadem,
     *Implicit Meanings: Essays in Anthropology* (London: Routledge and Paul, 1975),
     148–9.

10   On abjection and laughter, see especially Critchley, *On Humour.*

11   Not least because of the subsequent writers on laughter whom he influenced,
     e.g. Koestler, A. *The Act of Creation* (New York: MacMillan, 1964).

12   Page references correspond to Crick's recent translation, not the German.

13   For a fuller account of the play element in culture, see the classic work
     of Huizinga, J. *Homo Ludens: a study of the play element in culture* (Boston:
     Beacon Press, 1950; first published in German, 1944); for a loving narrative
     of the development of laughter in the infant, see Darwin, C. "A Biographical
     Sketch of an Infant," *Mind* 2 (1877), 288–9.

14   John Carey's introduction to the Penguin translation, however, thinks of the
     invocation of childhood as simply muddled (xx–xxi).

15   These quotes are from the last two paragraphs of Freud, S. "Humour", in
     *Collected Papers* vol. 5, ed. James Strachey (London/New York: The Psycho-
     Analytical Press, 1950).

16   Kofman, S. *Pourquoi rit-on? Freud et le mot d'esprit* (Paris: Éditions galilée,
     1986).

17   *Pourquoi rit-on?* 52.

18   The two versions are pp. 68 (the one quoted here) and 194 in the Crick
     translation of *The Joke.*

19   Isaak, J. *Feminism and Contemporary Art. The Revolutionary Power of Women's
     Laughter* (London: Routledge, 1996), 46.

20   Analyzed in detail in Conybeare, C. "The Ambiguous Laughter of Saint
     Laurence," *Journal of Early Christian Studies* 10 (2002), 175–202; see also
     Barton, C. "Savage Miracles: The Redemption of Lost Honor in Roman
     Society and the Sacrament of the Gladiator and the Martyr," *Representations*
     45 (1994), 41–71.

21   Freud's favorite joke may be said to elicit laughter of this kind: that of the
     man about to be hanged who observes blithely, "Well, the week's getting off
     to a good start." Discussed in Freud, S. "Humour".

DOI: 10.1057/9781137370914

**22**  Sully, J. *An Essay on Laughter*, 408.

**23**  Though the book is a novel, the brutal murder of Till – in 1955, at the age of fourteen – is not fictional.

**24**  Morrison, T. *Song of Solomon* (New York: Random House, 1977), 82.

**25**  Ellison, R. "An Extravagance of Laughter," in *Going to the Territory* (New York: Random House, 1986), 146. This is essay is discussed by Parvalescu, *Laughter: Notes on a Passion*, ch. 2, with due emphasis on the defiance implicit in insisting on this laughter.

**26**  Consider also the work of Donna Goldstein, an anthropological study sited in a *favela* of Rio de Janeiro: "The women I knew often joked and laughed about child death, rape, and murder...."; "This laughter was mad and absurd, similar to the conditions under which they lived": *Laughter Out of Place: Race, Class, Violence, and Sexuality in a Rio Shantytown* (Berkeley/Los Angeles/London: University of California Press, 2003), 45 and 39.

**27**  Critchley, S. *Infinitely Demanding: Ethics of Commitment, Politics of Resistance* (London/New York: Verso, 2007), 82 (Critchley's emphasis). Compare Lippitt on Kierkegaard and Nietzsche: "for both..., humour and laughter operate as *expressions of the limitations of human possibility*," Lippitt, J. "Existential Laughter", *Cogito* 10 (1996), 70 (Lippitt's emphasis).

DOI: 10.1057/9781137370914

# 4
# Laughter and the Body

Abstract: *This is the second chapter analyzing the theories about laughter of major twentieth-century thinkers, this time those who place at the center of their theory the situation of laughter in the body, and the relationship between laughter and embodied experience. Here I deal with Mikhail Bakhtin, and his theories of carnivalesque laughter, the "true ambivalent and universal laughter" that destroys and renews. This leads to a critique of the "universal" as appropriate to laughter, and thence to a lesser-known thinker, Helmut Plessner, who situates laughter at the point of tension between the human as "embodied" and as "in the body" – that is, between subjective and objective experience. Again, while both may contribute to an appreciation of the quality of Sarah's laughter, neither is satisfactory to describe it.*

Conybeare, Catherine. *The Laughter of Sarah: Biblical Exegesis, Feminist Theory, and the Concept of Delight.* New York: Palgrave Macmillan, 2013.
DOI: 10.1057/9781137370914.

DOI: 10.1057/9781137370914

Laughter, then, is wont to engage power dynamics, both those of superiority and those of inferiority; but these types of laughter, and the theories that account for them, do not seem to capture the laughter that is our subject here. So for illumination, we shall turn to the other principal division of theories about laughter, those which are grounded in the relationship between laughter and the body.

While I am provisionally expressing these dynamics as those of power and those of the body, another way of putting it might be as the external and internal dynamics of laughter: those which relate to the outside world and the people around one, and those which relate to laughter's physical production, its production from within the body. Clearly, this is not a sharp division; the two blend into each other. The laughing subject, the person who laughs, is situated amid other people, laughing and not. Nonetheless, my division draws out the emphases in different accounts.

The work of Mikhail Bakhtin is an essential contribution to thinking about laughter's association with the body. The influence of Bakhtin's discussion of laughter and his notion of the carnivalesque, as developed in *Rabelais and His World*, has been out of all proportion to the specificity of his sphere of interest: Bakhtin's work is essentially a study of Rabelais, and of the relation of Rabelais to medieval "folk culture." Bakhtin argues that Rabelais – and, to a lesser degree, Cervantes and Shakespeare – produced their work at an exceptional moment when "popular-festive laughter," the counter-institutional laughter of the Feast of Fools and other "alternative" feast days of the Middle Ages, was incorporated seamlessly into high literary endeavor.[1] Laughter is characterized by universalism, freedom, and its relation to the "people's unofficial truth" (*Rabelais* 90 and passim); it represents "victory over fear" and "uncrowning and renewal, a gay transformation" (91); it "create[s] no dogmas" (95). The attitude of this Renaissance moment was, according to Bakhtin, that "certain essential aspects of the world are accessible only to laughter" (66). But by the seventeenth century describing a literary work as "amusing and gay" had come to mean it was "low and irrelevant" (65), and by the Enlightenment, the "principle of laughter" had been cut down to "cold humor, irony, sarcasm" (38). (Rabelais, says Bakhtin, is particularly misunderstood by Voltaire.)[2]

The disproportionate influence of Bakhtin derives, I think, from the fact that he had the courage to set down in writing an agglomeration of properties of laughter that we feel instinctively to be apt, but that are hard to ground in the conventions of academic discourse and attribution.

DOI: 10.1057/9781137370914

Moreover, he gazes unflinching at the sources of laughter that may disgust a contemporary sensibility – there is a lot of pissing and shitting in Rabelais, and a lot of outlandish penises – and shows how they are related to the simultaneous debasement and renewal afforded by the carnival spirit and marked by laughter.

Bakhtin insists on the association of laughter with "the body's lower stratum" (*Rabelais* 55), which itself is associated with "fertility, growth, and a brimming-over abundance" (19). This, in turn, serves to associate laughter particularly with women:

> woman is essentially related to the material bodily lower stratum; she is the *incarnation* of this stratum that degrades and regenerates simultaneously. She is ambivalent. She debases, brings down to earth, lends a bodily substance to things, and destroys; but, first of all, she is the principle that gives birth. (240)

This is very much the instinct voiced fifteen hundred years earlier by Augustine. He responds to Aristotle's claim, cited in my prologue, that laughter is unique to humanity, by grumbling that "whoever judges rightly about human nature certainly thinks that it [laughter] is human, but the lowest part of the human."[3] Given that elsewhere, Augustine makes it quite clear that "the lowest part of the human" is also the female part,[4] we can see that laughter has across the centuries been associated with a distasteful bodiliness which is typified as female. Part of Bakhtin's insight is to try to make that bodiliness not distasteful, but valuable, indeed essential to human thriving; but his sense of its value is, as we shall see, mediated and qualified.

Bakhtin's notion of laughter is simultaneously very specific and very general. It is specific to what he reads in Rabelais, and to a putative notion of "carnival" in late medieval practice, which slips between the popular celebrations surrounding great church festivals and, more loosely, "the varied popular-festive life" of the middle ages (218). The general aspect is expressed throughout the book in sweeping claims about "true ambivalent and universal laughter" (versions of this at e.g. 11; 82), the sense of "universal" relating generally to the objects of laughter, "directed at the wholeness of the world." In the end, medieval laughter is not "subjective, individual," but "the social consciousness of all the people" (92), "a free weapon in [the people's] hands" (94).

There is a dark undercurrent to the specificity, which seems driven by what Bakhtin finds in Rabelais. The womb is repeatedly described as

DOI: 10.1057/9781137370914

"the bodily grave" of man (92, 241) – hence the womanly stratum that "degrades and regenerates simultaneously." There is little explanation of the association of womb with grave, and to sustain that image one would need a word with the ambiguity of the Latin *venter*, which means both "womb" and "stomach," and then to consider the stomach the "grave" of food. And yet in Russian, there is no such ambiguity: the word for womb, *matka*, derives from the word for mother.[5] How can it be that something whose function is to generate and nurture life is so persistently associated with death?

There is also a persistent valuing of violence as part of carnival laughter, including the paradoxical notion of "bridal creative blows" (205): "Every blow dealt to the old helps the new to be born. The Caesarian operation kills the mother but delivers the child." (That this association of ideas can work at all for Bakhtin shows again how deeply compromised the idea of the body, and the bodiliness of laughter, remains.) Passages of Rabelais are indeed graphically violent; Bakhtin argues that it is through their very excess, and through the space that they open for renewal, that they generate laughter. But when Friar John initiates a massacre to protect his monastery's vineyards, can he really be said to be changing blood into wine?[6] Must laughter and humanity necessarily be so antipathetic to each other?

The root of the problem, however, lies in the claims of universalism. By this I mean collapsing the laughter of individual persons into "the people," not the notion of the universal that Bakhtin relates to the objects of laughter. What does it mean for laughter to yield up its particularity – the individual who laughs, the individual thing laughed at – for some general group expression? This sounds perilously close to the responses of the mob, however carefully the laughter is related to freedom. Moreover, it is not clear who "the people" are whose laugh is being championed.[7] Is this a truly universal category (whatever that might mean) – or is this a group opposed to the authority figures of church and state against which the carnival is presumptively a rebellion?[8] Often, it sounds like the latter: "the verbal norms of official and literary language, determined by the canon, prohibit all that is linked with fecundation, pregnancy, childbirth" (320). But if we think of the example of Sarah's laughter, it is indissolubly linked with childbirth; and Genesis is nothing if not canonical. Bakhtin's premise of the universal collective nature of laughter is in fact built on a problematic and shifting binary:[9] the universal is all those who, in a given instance, are caught up in the carnival spirit – and who laugh, delighting in degradation, at the "upper stratum" of effete authority.

DOI: 10.1057/9781137370914

Consider when this book was written: there is something gallant about its dogged assertion of universal human value – for Bakhtin takes his genealogy of laughter all the way back to Aristotle – against the background of Stalinist Russia; about its faith in laughter as the unassailably true expression of the free human spirit. ("The principle of laughter…frees human consciousness, thought, and imagination for new potentialities," 49.) Although the book was published after Stalin's death, the ideas were developed in the context of his increasingly terrifying totalitarian rule.[10] And although the book's nostalgic retrojection of popular ebullition onto Rabelais and his medieval predecessors, and the generalizations on which it depends, seem in many ways ill-founded, there is much that I would like to bring to my analysis of the laughter of delight.

This involves to some degree reading against the grain of Bakhtin: for he insists that we must be attentive to the specifics of laughter in a given historical moment;[11] and, however true it is that the causes and contexts of laughter – the occasions for laughter – may change at different moments in time, I would like to highlight some aspects of his theory that seem to me to resonate diachronically. Bakhtin's notion of the openness of laughter to the world – its universality in that sense – seems to me hugely important: that laughter is open to anything, may embrace anything. Related to this is his refusal to sub-divide laughter into suitable and unsuitable contexts – to hive off the frivolous from the serious – and his insistence on laughter's "multiplicity of meaning" (109, 140). And although in its particulars I find Bakhtin's association of laughter with the body quite vexed, that he insists on the association as such is essential.[12]

The vexation comes with Bakhtin's ongoing association of laughter with the violence done to the bodies of both women and men, and with his association of women's bodies with death, swallowing, and decay, as well as with the origins of life. But this leads directly to the question of whether – if we emphasize that laughter is situated in the body – laughter should be associated more particularly with the bodies of women than of men. Are women particularly prone to laughter? And, more specifically, to the laughter of delight?

On the one hand, no. A claim in this context to women's special propensity for laughter simply replicates the age-old association of women with body as against the association of men with intellect or soul. The reasoning would go, laughter is bodily, so women are particularly prone to laughter. Since I reject the dichotomous contrast of women/body to

DOI: 10.1057/9781137370914

men/intellect, I would also reject the notion that laughter should be situated uniquely or preferentially in a female body. There is no necessary or fixed relation between gender and laughter: the laughing subject may be both female and male.

In another way, we should answer yes. Once we take into account their socio-cultural context – as we must – women may be more particularly associated with laughter. But not, unfortunately, with the laughter of delight. I would think rather of the dynamics of laughter as a coping mechanism that I explored briefly in the previous chapter. The laughter of delight may bubble up in a body of either gender – perhaps I should say, of any gender – since, however that body may be conditioned by circumstance or expectation, it need simply be open to a momentary joy.

To return to Bakhtin, an important corollary of his recognition that laughter is situated in the body is his insistence on the social aspect of laughter. Visualizing a body living amid other bodies, we become concerned with who hears the laughter, who is implicated, who may be participating in or resisting the laughter. One laughing subject engenders others; laughter is contagious.[13]

Laughter, indeed, creates a fleeting community of those who hear it, whether or not they are drawn into participation. The openness of the laughing subject, the way in which she engages the world, makes some sort of response almost inevitable. We may recall the dramatic episode from Midrash, cited in chapter 1, when Abraham tells Sarah to uncover her breasts: "she uncovered her breasts and the milk gushed forth as from two fountains, and noble ladies came and had their children suckled by her." This literal, startling uncovering, the fountains of milk gushing from Sarah's breasts – vividly present, unavoidable – is like the uncovering of her emotions in her triumphant delighted laughter. Whether we watch or look away, whether we are drawn in or refuse, we are responding. And in fact, we cannot fully refuse laughter, for our ears cannot be fully closed to it; laughter will inevitably engage those who can hear it.

A recent collection of essays looks at this phenomenon – the creation of *Lachgemeinschaften*, communities of laughter, through these transient "social events."[14] *Lachgemeinschaften* may of course take sinister, mocking, or exclusionary form, just as laughter itself may do;[15] but they may also be communities, albeit fleeting ones, of shared delight.[16] The emphasis is on laughter as a form of social communication, dynamic and processual; the editors draw on the work of the anthropologist Mary Douglas to show that this may also be an anti-hierarchical form of communication – or

DOI: 10.1057/9781137370914

perhaps better expressed, a communication without hierarchy: Douglas writes of community, in the sense of "unhierarchized undifferentiated social relations," being well expressed by laughter and jokes.[17] This is not Bakhtinian inversion we are talking about, but the momentary dissolution of hierarchies altogether. In the shared capitulation to a moment of involuntary laughter, all those in the *Lachgemeinschaft* are equal.

This recalls us, however, to the complexities of laughter and community. The "shared capitulation" is momentary; and for all that it represents a moment of joyous communication, it does not erase particularity. To put it another way, the individual is opened up to the laughter, temporarily dissolved; but individuality remains. One of the most pressing critiques of laughter as a generalized concept is that, yet again, it draws laughter away from the individual person laughing, and hence begins to empty the laughter of meaning. It is not that we cannot envisage, or rather "hear," the laughter of a multitude, but that we must remain aware that this multitude is composed of specific instances of laughter, of specific people laughing.

It is impossible to imagine laughter without a person doing the laughing. The laughing person may be temporarily out of sight or altogether invisible; but once we hear the sound of laughter, we need to imagine a body producing that sound and, arguably, an entire context in which it is produced. So there must always be a body that laughs. Think of the delightful absurdity of Lewis Carroll's Cheshire cat: "[the Cat] vanished quite slowly, beginning with the end of the tail, and ending with the grin, which remained some time after the rest of it had gone."[18] The logician in Carroll is playing with the notion that it is impossible for the grin to persist after the body has gone.

One scholar who discusses particularly well the dependency of laughter on the body is Helmuth Plessner. He ought to make a fourth in the group of great twentieth-century thinkers on laughter – Bergson, Freud, Bakhtin – whose work I have already discussed; but, for whatever reason of historical accident or fashion, his work on laughter has tended to be overlooked.[19] And yet Plessner's theory of laughter is more encompassing than the others', and his book, *Laughing and Crying* (originally published in 1941 as *Lachen und Weinen*), deserves to be considered a classic. Plessner is the only one among this distinguished quartet of laughter theorists whose notion of laughter has the potential to embrace the laugh of delight. "The lightness achieved, and at the same time tempered, by insight into the real unmanageability in the essence of things

DOI: 10.1057/9781137370914

is the best climate for a laughter that surges up from within," he writes (72) – and, though he does not mention the biblical episode, he could be thinking of Sarah. Plessner is also the only one of the four who makes laughter's situation in the body a central part of his account. Indeed, in an explicitly anti-Cartesian mode, he writes of his work as "philosophical anthropology," which neatly illustrates the way in which he conceives it as spanning mind and body.

Plessner's great insight is to link the eruption of laughter to what he calls the human being's "eccentric" relation to his or her own body:[20] "the situation of my existence is ambiguous: *as* physical lived body – *in* the physical lived body" (36). In other words, the human is both an "embodied" (*leibhaften*) creature and a creature "in the body" (*im Körpen*) (32), simultaneously aware of its own subjective animated existence and of itself from the outside, as an object. And it is when the human being comes up against that fundamental ambiguity of existence that he or she responds – according to circumstance – by laughing or crying. Plessner's account is all about gaps, between-ness, friction between different modes, norms, levels of existence (78, 87), and above all about the permanent, hopeless, yet bewitching incommensurability of body and soul.[21]

Plessner develops his account of laughter as fundamentally embodied by pondering its relationship to meaning. In laughing and crying, man responds to something *with his body as body* – in a manner irreducible to symbolic form (31). Indeed, in the closing pages of his book Plessner goes so far as to argue that this response occurs when confronted with the "boundaries of the not-sensical," the non-negotiable fact of man's eccentric relationship with his own body, which is "necessarily opaque" (156). So what can we say about laughter's irreducibility to symbolic form – that is, to conventional constructions of meaning? Plessner explores, and dismisses, the possibility that laughter is a sort of gesture. Laughter, he argues, despite being corporeally expressed, is not part of the language of gesture: its consistent instantiation across time and place, its involuntary, even compulsive nature, and its lack of conscious signification all militate against that (51). Gesture, by contrast, is culturally specific, willed, and conveys articulable meaning that is present to the conscious self. And yet laughter is essentially, directly, expressive: "Irreplaceability, immediacy, and involuntariness give laughter and crying the character of true expressive movements" (56).[22] Plessner is also laudably attentive to the surroundings in which the laughter takes place: "*the loss of control in the whole context* has expressive value"; "the effective impossibility of

DOI: 10.1057/9781137370914

finding a suitable expression and an appropriate answer *is* at the same time the only suitable expression, the only appropriate answer" (66; Plessner's italics). In involuntariness and aporia lie the conditions for laughter; and here we find the basis for a pressing link between the emotions and laughter, for Plessner makes clear that laughter is, essentially, expressive of emotions that cannot find another outlet.

There are oddities in Plessner's account of laughter. Once he begins to discuss specific "occasions of laughter" (his third chapter) he is beholden to both Freud and Bergson in ways that seem inconsistent with his general observations about the dynamics of laughter. For example, he writes that "the laughing person is open to the world" – but immediately reneges on that openness with talk of disengagement and "self-distance," which echoes Bergson's claim that laughter is divorced from the emotions (115). Plessner talks of the gaps in "our technique of taking the world seriously and binding it to us" (92) which give occasion for laughter – but the agency presupposed by "binding" forms an odd juxtaposition with his insistence on our ongoing and inevitable awareness of our "eccentric" relationship with our bodies. In the end, Plessner creates what seems to me a false antithesis between laughter and crying which leads him to insist on the "superficiality" of laughter – because crying, by contrast, is profound – and on the notion that a person "doesn't really laugh; there is laughter in him," while he truly participates in his own crying (116). In the end, laughter is somehow impersonal, for Plessner; crying is personal.

Perhaps the shift in ground is due to the circumstances of composition and publication of Plessner's book – as I mentioned, it came out in 1941, at which time Plessner was in exile from his native Germany; perhaps he was progressively losing faith in the possibility of laughter truly rooted in the human body. That is certainly the trajectory of the book itself. But large parts of *Laughing and Crying* suggest the opposite: that laughter is deeply personal and specific; that it is at the same time always embedded in a wider context; that it expresses a fundamental openness to that context, to "the world"; and that what it expresses is specific to the occasion and inexpressible in any other form. When he writes that "the effective impossibility of finding a suitable expression and an appropriate answer *is* at the same time the only suitable expression, the only appropriate answer" (66), he could be thinking of the laughter of Sarah. Or, for that matter, of Abraham. You will remember from chapter 1 that, according to John Chrysostom, Abraham "fell on his face and laughed" at God's promise of a son not because he didn't believe the promise, but because

DOI: 10.1057/9781137370914

he didn't have anything to say, *ouk echōn ho ti eipei*: being beyond words, expressing the impossibility of expression.[23]

We can reach back well before the twentieth century to think about the idiosyncratic relationship between laughter and the body. There is a marvelous sixteenth-century treatise on laughter by the physician Laurent Joubert. Joubert, indeed, provides an important part of the intellectual context in which Hobbes develops his theory of laughter;[24] but Joubert's account is much less judgemental. He works from the starting point of a physiological account of laughter to produce a total account of the phenomenon of laughter in the human being. Though the study is well-larded with quotations from writers ranging from ancient times to his own, Joubert's primary attention remains directed to the corporeal aspects of laughter – and they prove to be a rich source of observation.

> Now among the things which suddenly and considerably move the body because they have first touched or moved the mind, laughable matter is not the least...Of the other passions there are hardly any signs that show up in the face, but from laughter how great and in what great number do they come, not only in the face but also in the entire body!...What increases the marvel is that something insignificant, completely foolish and light, is able to move the mind in such great agitation, and even more, the fact that laughter escapes so suddenly and promptly, and obeys reason and the will less than any other emotion, although it excites all these gestures by means of the very muscles which serve the will![25]

Here, beautifully expressed, is the weird conjunction of body and mind, of the involuntary and the willed, involved in laughter. Laughter is described as an emotion of sorts, but an emotion *sui generis*, the power of its existence inferred from its powerful bodily manifestation. And, like Sarah's laughter in Chrysostom's account, Joubert's emerges suddenly – *athroon* – and challenges conventional measures of time and response.

Having said this, I should add that Joubert's notion of what prompts laughter ultimately derives from Aristotle: that it is compounded of "ugliness" – or deficiency – and "absence of strong emotion." Although I would like an account of the laughter of delight to comprehend what is, in the words of Joubert, "completely foolish and light," I think it also may be prompted by "strong emotion."

For if the involuntary nature of the laughter is important, so too is a certain emotional engagement. Against all insistence to the contrary – the

DOI: 10.1057/9781137370914

canard that intellect and emotions must be separate, and that laughter only engages the former – the *Lachgemeinschaft* created by delight will involve a generous emotional openness in each individual. It is not just about thinking; it is about feeling as well. How is it that studies of laughter have constantly refused to accept this involvement of the emotions? I think it is because of the focus on the mental aspects of laughter – the apprehension of the jokes, verbally or visually enacted, that prompt it. Certainly that is the case with Freud and Bergson – representing respectively the verbal and the visual emphasis. Paradoxically, the emphasis on mental triggers for laughter results in an externalist view of laughter – laughter looked at from the outside, analyzed as a pattern of response, either disembodied or (as in Freud's account) so metaphorically, abstractly embodied as to lose sight of the actual person who is laughing. But to think about the person, the embodied laughing subject, is immediately to capture laughter's engagement with the emotions as well as with external stimuli.[26] Introducing subjectivity to laughter shows more clearly the complex network of internal and external factors on which laughter depends. Laughter is – in a sense – at once in and not in the body. This is what Plessner sees so well. Getting, in imagination, *inside* the laughing subject is crucial for appreciating the laughter of delight.

The complicated relationship between the laughing subject and laughter itself is summed up in Alter's inspired and ambiguous rendering of Sarah's cry: "Laughter has God made me." Is Sarah the one doing the laughing, or is she the object of laughter? Has she actually in some sense become laughter? Is the laughter also a personification, a reference to Isaac? Or is it all of these? The simultaneous affirmation and dissolution of the subject in laughter is a fundamental part of the nature of laughter. The affirmation comes because laughter is utterly peculiar to the individual: laughter will strike no two people in exactly the same way. The dissolution comes in the apparent melting of boundaries, both within and without the laughing subject: people laughing together have an overpowering sense of unity, even as they are themselves overpowered by their own laughter. They are indeed, in a sense, "made laughter."

# Notes

1    Bakhtin makes this argument in spite of the fact – which he mentions – that the contemporary institutions of culture roundly rejected Rabelais: Rabelais

DOI: 10.1057/9781137370914

narrowly escaped charges of heresy, and his books were condemned by the Sorbonne – whence, no doubt, the marvelous parody of academic fakery in *Gargantua* intr./ann. G. Defaux (Paris: Librairie Générale Française, 1994; first published 1535), chapter 18.

2   Bakhtin quotes Voltaire's commentary: "Rabelais in his extravagant and unintelligible book let loose an extreme jollity and an extreme impertinence; he poured out erudition, filth and boredom; you will get a good story two pages long, at the price of two volumes of nonsense," Bakhtin, M. *Rabelais and His World* tr. H. Iswolsky (Cambridge, MA: MIT Press, 1968; first published in Russian, 1965), 116–17.

3   *humanum quidem, sed infimum hominis iudicat, quisquis de natura humana rectissime iudicat*: Augustine, *De Libero Arbitrio* ed. W. M. Green, CCL 29 (Turnhout 1970), 1.8.

4   For example, consider this passage, from Augustine's first commentary on Genesis against the Manichaeans: "... woman was created, and the order of things subjugates her to the man – so that what is clearly apparent in two individual people, i.e. man and woman, might also be discerned in a single person: that the inner mind, like masculine reason [*virilis ratio*] might keep the appetite of the spirit ... subjugated, and by a balanced rule might impose moderation on the appetite with its own help – just as man should rule woman, and not let her dominate the man (when that happens, it is a wretched, perverted household)," Augustine, *De Genesi contra Manichaeos* ed. D. Weber, CSEL 91 (Vienna 1998), 2.11.15.

5   Thanks to my colleague at Bryn Mawr, Sharon Bain, for this information.

6   *Gargantua*, Chapter 27; discussed in Bakhtin *Rabelais*, 208–9.

7   *Rabelais*, 12: "The people's ambivalent laughter ... expresses the point of view of the whole world. ..."

8   This is clearly a critique that was vigorously pursued in the USSR in Bakhtin's time: though most of it is untranslated, and I cannot read Russian, the tip of an interpretative iceberg is, I think, found in Gourévitch, A. "Le comique et le sérieux dans la littérature religieuse du moyen age", *Diogène* 90 (1975), 67–89, which builds on the work of Olga Friedenberg.

9   Critiqued in some detail in Lachmann, R. "Bakhtin and Carnival: Culture as Counter-Culture," *Cultural Critique* 11 (Winter, 1988–9), 115–52, 128–31: "The rationality of Bakhtin's carnival is decentered ... It is a rationality of doubling."

10  See Emerson, C. "Coming to Terms with Bakhtin's Carnival: Ancient, Modern, sub Specie Aeternitatis," in *Bakhtin and the Classics* ed. R. Bracht Branham (Evanston, IL: Northwestern University Press, 2002), 5–26, on the complexity of interpreting the historical context against which *Rabelais* was written, and on Bakhtin's own compromised circumstances at the time (11, 17).

DOI: 10.1057/9781137370914

11    See, for example, Bakhtin's observation that if laughter in Rabelais is read as "nonhistorical and unchanging," one will miss its pervasiveness (*Rabelais*, 134–5).

12    Compare Bakhtin's marvelous observation on games: that they "uncrown gloomy eschatological time" and "renew time on the material bodily level" (*Rabelais*, 238). As will be seen, this is one of the trajectories I am tracing for laughter.

13    Work has been done on the strange phenomenon of "epidemics" of laughter: references in Provine, R. R. "Laughter", *American Scientist* 84:1 (1996). But I mean something less pathologized: Lloyd Morgan writes, charmingly, of the "beneficent contagiousness" of laughter: Lloyd Morgan, C. "Laughter", in *Encyclopaedia of Religion and Ethics* vol. VII (New York/Edinburgh: Charles Scribner's Sons, 1915).

14    Röcke, W., and H. R. Velten (eds.) *Lachgemeinschaften. Kulturelle Inszenierungen und soziale Wirkungen von Gelächter im Mittelalter und in der Frühen Neuzeit* Trends in Medieval Philology 4 (Berlin/New York 2005); the notion builds on Brian Stock's "textual communities," first proposed in *The Implications of Literacy: Written Language and Models of Interpretation in the Eleventh and Twelfth Centuries* (Princeton: Princeton University Press, 1983), but developed particularly in Stock, B. *Listening for the Text: On the Uses of the Past* (Philadelphia: University of Pennsylvania Press, 1990), Chapter 7, "Textual communities."

15    For extended sociolinguistic analysis of the phenomenon, see e.g. Glenn, P. *Laughter in Interaction* Studies in Interactional Sociolinguistics (Cambridge: Cambridge University Press, 2003).

16    Such communities have been provisionally explored in Rosenwein, B. *Emotional Communities in the Early Middle Ages* (Ithaca and London: Cornell University Press, 2006).

17    Douglas, M. "Jokes," in eadem, *Implicit Meanings: Essays in Anthropology* (London: Routledge and Paul, 1975); quote from p. 156. Note, however, that this is just one part of a multifaceted set of instances of the functioning of jokes in different social contexts.

18    *Alice's Adventures in Wonderland*, Chapter 6.

19    Simon Critchley's work is an exception; see also Prusak's eloquent project of recovery in "The Science of Laughter: Helmuth Plessner's *Laughing and Crying* revisited," *Continental Philosophy Review* 38 (2006), 41–69.

20    In Plessner's thought, undoubtedly *his* body: he is regrettably dismissive of "woman" – who "matures earlier than man, but seldom gets as far as he," and who "has a comparatively childlike, elemental nature," 121.

21    Bakhtin too entertained – in writings other than *Rabelais* – a notion of the eccentricity of the self; though this does not relate to the body-soul dichotomy, but to looking at oneself as if from outside. See Lachmann,

DOI: 10.1057/9781137370914

"Bakhtin and Carnival," 152; Emerson, C. "Coming to Terms with Bakhtin's Carnival," 8–9.

22  Contradicted, for crying, in Plessner's conclusions: "Openness, immediacy, eruptivity characterize laughter; closure, mediacy, gradualness characterize crying" (146).

23  John Chrysostom, *Homiliae in Genesim*, 40 (*PG* 53, col. 370). The passage goes on to say that, because of his own age and her sterility, he was "at a loss, and astounded at the promise of God."

24  See Skinner, Q. "Hobbes and the classical theory of laughter," in idem, *Visions of Politics* vol. 3 (Cambridge: Cambridge University Press, 2002), 142–76; Bakhtin also uses Joubert: *Rabelais*, 68–70.

25  Joubert, L. *Treatise on Laughter* tr. De Rocher (Tuscaloosa, AL: University of Alabama Press, 1980; first published in French, 1579), 71.

26  Studies on tickling babies show that even they will laugh far more readily when tickled by someone they know and trust: a perfect example of the necessary conjunction of emotional factors with physiological stimulus. Note, by the way, that Aristotle's original, much-cited *aperçu* about laughter (*Part. An.* 673a8) is actually in the context of a discussion of tickling.

DOI: 10.1057/9781137370914

# 5
# Laughter, Volatility, Instability

Abstract: *In the final three chapters of the book, I use a range of contemporary theorists to explore how to "hear" the laughter of delight, and what the consequences of that hearing might be. The theories are loosely grouped around the Arendtian notion of "natality," which draws out the philosophical significance of birth, as opposed to the more conventional preoccupation with death. This chapter looks again at the relationship of laughter to the body, using theorists ranging from Hannah Arendt to Alenka Zupančič: it considers the radical instability of laughter, linked to that of the body, and the way in which the self may be dissolved, undone, in laughter.*

Conybeare, Catherine. *The Laughter of Sarah: Biblical Exegesis, Feminist Theory, and the Concept of Delight.* New York: Palgrave Macmillan, 2013.
DOI: 10.1057/9781137370914.

As soon as we invoke the body, rather than some idealized abstraction, things become messy. Productively messy, I hope. It is a given that the body – the corporeal – is fluctuating and unstable; the question becomes, how do we value that instability? Moreover, I keep talking about specificity: how does that fit in when we are talking about a fluctuating entity? And what about agency? When a body laughs, who or what is really doing the laughing?

Back in chapter 1, Basil of Caesarea warned, "Let the ambiguity (*homōnymia*) of laughter not mislead us."[1] *Homōnymia* suggests the calling of different things or properties by the same name; and indeed, by now we can see that for laughter we need a term fuller than "ambiguity," which in its origins only suggests a spanning of two possible meanings. We need something that embraces the many possibilities inherent in the notion of laughter. Besides, we can go one step further: the ambiguity of the term "laughter" is engendered by an essential ambiguity in the nature of laughter itself. It is not just that "laughter" covers a multitude of different phenomena, that in any given instance are clear and stable entities; the phenomenon "laughter" is itself multitudinous – or, better put, polysemous. It is of its very nature associated with shifting, flowing, mutating dynamics.

There is a wide range of evidence for the multivalence of laughter, for example, in the recent compendious study of Greek laughter by Stephen Halliwell. Halliwell adverts repeatedly to the ambiguity, or instability, or volatility, at the heart of laughter: he writes of the Greeks' "awareness of the difficulty of pinning down the volatile workings of laughter" (11) and of the "instabilities that inhere in laughter itself" (73, echoed e.g. at 140, 237). These "instabilities" relate to laughter's association "with both positive... and negative... emotions, with (innocent) 'play' and socially disruptive aggression, with the taking of pleasure and the giving of pain, with the affirmation of life and the fear of death" (11) – in other words, with the whole gamut of meaning which we have found in the Hebrew *tseḥoq* as well as the Greek *gelōs*. (The Latin *risus* covers smiling as well as laughter, and so is in some ways even more "unstable.") Halliwell tracks the instabilities not only in the manifestations of laughter that he documents, but also in their causes and their interpretation: the instability pertains not just to the laughter itself, but to the person laughing and the audience for the laughter. It is clear that laughter not only oscillates from "positive" to "negative" between occasions, but even within the same occasion; and that it may be experienced very differently in a given

DOI: 10.1057/9781137370914

instance by laugher and hearer. Even "oscillation" seems too corporeal, too mechanical an image to use.

The initial laughter of Abraham and Sarah at the annunciation of Isaac's birth plays out this instability of meaning when read alongside the patristic interpretations of their laughter. Their two outbursts in the biblical account are barely differentiated from each other. Compare "And Abraham flung himself on his face and he laughed, saying to himself, 'To a hundred-year-old will a child be born, will ninety-year-old Sarah give birth?'" (Gen. 17:17) with "And Sarah laughed inwardly, saying, 'After being shriveled, shall I have pleasure, and my husband is old?'" (Gen. 18:12). Each is a complex, private response to miraculous news; each, one might argue, expresses doubtful amusement that the impossible has been predicted. And yet the interpretations of their meaning, as we saw in chapter 1, vary widely, and often do venture to differentiate between the two instances. Laughter is of its very nature an unstable vessel of meaning.

It seems almost incredible that laughter maintains a distinct identity, occupies a distinct category, in the midst of this radical instability. But clearly, the "instability" of laughter is somehow a crucial part of what makes laughter itself.[2] What happens if we press on this instability? What do we discover, in the recognition and exploration of the multivalence of laughter?

Instability and multivalence are not, of course, identical concepts. One may in theory encounter multivalence without instability: a multitude of meanings which yet do not slither into each other. But we cannot embrace instability without embracing multivalence as well.

The beginnings of a way into this question are suggested by a book published more than half a century ago, Simone de Beauvoir's *The Ethics of Ambiguity*. This work starts from the desire to defend Sartre's existentialism as ethical, or rather to provide an ethics for his existentialism; but Beauvoir's thought quickly takes on a life of its own. The "ambiguity" of the title is initially defined as the human experience of "being a sovereign and unique subject amidst a universe of objects" while being "in turn an object for others" – that is, other people, each of whom experiences him or herself as a "sovereign and unique subject" (7). (We are reminded of Plessner and his observation that a human being is simultaneously both "embodied" and "in the body.") Beauvoir's description of the "sovereign and unique subject" is at odds with the notion of laughter that I am developing, and I shall address it directly below. However, her

DOI: 10.1057/9781137370914

characterization of the individual grounds her notion of ambiguity: it is that which is important here.

As Beauvoir's thought develops, in the course of *The Ethics of Ambiguity*, she imparts a rich sense of the possibilities of dwelling in ambiguity – the ambiguity inherent in life in the world. Process and imperfectibility are crucial; so is failure, which is associated with freedom (138).[3] (It is interesting how post-lapsarian this formulation is: theologically speaking, free will is justified because it bestows the ability to choose the right course – but it also, of course, bestows the possibility of wrong choices and failure.) The individual human being is valued, and so is the specificity of human relations, while "mankind" is suspect (157). "Morality resides in the painfulness of an indefinite questioning," writes Beauvoir (133); the Augustine of the *Confessions* would agree.[4] Above all, in a pointed critique of Marxism, "production and wealth ... have meaning only if they are capable of being retrieved in individual and living joy. The saving of time and the conquest of leisure have no meaning if we are not moved by the laugh of a child at play" (135).

It is joy and laughter that, for Beauvoir, bring meaning to the brute mechanics of existence. "If we do not love life on our own account and through others, it is futile to seek to justify it in any way" (136). When she writes of laughter, she is not addressing the ambiguity of laughter *per se*, but the laughter that recognizes ambiguity, explicitly or not. "The ambiguity of freedom ... introduces a difficult equivocation into relationships with each individual taken one by one" (136). The "laugh of a child at play" expresses that freedom, and for us to pause and delight in the laughter is for us to revel in "the ambiguity of freedom." Laughter celebrates being in the world, with all its absurdities and apparent paradoxes.[5] And yet – this is my addition, not Beauvoir's – the ambiguity or, as we have been calling it, the instability of laughter itself is symptomatic of these worldly ambiguities.

There is a delightful passage in Augustine's correspondence that recognizes the permeability of laughter to the "worldly ambiguities" approved by Beauvoir. It comes in the course of a letter to a much-admired contemporary, social superior, and prominent convert to ascetic Christianity, Paulinus of Nola. Earlier, Augustine has asked Paulinus a number of questions about the afterlife, and Paulinus has responded, rather unhelpfully, that he would prefer not to address them, since he is kept sufficiently busy trying to work out how to live well in his present life. Not to be discouraged, Augustine continues by asking Paulinus:

DOI: 10.1057/9781137370914

how one should live either among or for those people [Augustine is a bishop, and concerned for his congregation] who don't yet know how to live by dying – dying not through escape from the body, but through [cultivating] the cast of mind that turns itself away from bodily delights. Generally it seems to me that, unless I fit myself a little to the very things from which I yearn to extricate those people, I shan't be able to do anything for their salvation. But when I do this, delight in such things creeps up on me, so that often even empty speech delights me, and I give ear to the speakers not just to smile but actually to be conquered and dissolved in laughter (*nec adridere tantum sed etiam risu uinci ac solui*). (*ep.* 95.2)

Here, succinctly expressed, is the very observation that we were making in chapter 2: that laughter is incompatible with a teleological world view, with a life lived turning "away from bodily delights," dying to worldly concerns and looking ahead to the end times, the "land of laughter" that is heaven. Augustine knows that ideologically he ought not to submit to worldly laughter – and yet at times he cannot resist.

What, then, should be the relation of the laughing subject to the world? This looks to the longstanding philosophical tension between contemplation and engagement. Beauvoir, for example, suggests that "an ethics of ambiguity will be one which will refuse to deny *a priori* that separate existants can, at the same time, be bound to each other, that their individual freedoms can forge laws valid for all" (18). The double negative is, I think, important: it is more cautious and provisional than outright affirmation, which suits the delicate interrelationship that Beauvoir is expressing; and it also evokes a philosophical tradition that *has* historically "den[ied] *a priori* that separate existants can, at the same time, be bound to each other."[6]

It is worth pausing for a moment over this notion, for it is historically significant; and it obviates the possibility of *Lachgemeinschaften*, which are one of the things that we have identified as an important component of laughter's mode of operation. The philosophical tradition toward which Beauvoir is glancing here is one that considers contemplation of the divine – or, in Plotinian terms, the One – to be the highest possible ethical endeavor; the solitary effort to achieve union with the divine trumps all the more relational values which recognize the body's being in society and association with others. The superiority of the solitary attempt at union explains, for example, the disjuncture between the discussion of *theoria* ("contemplation") in the final book of Aristotle's *Nicomachean Ethics* from all that came before it, particularly the work's

DOI: 10.1057/9781137370914

rich appreciation of the ethical value of friendship. It also explains the idealized account of Plotinus' philosophical practice given by his awe-struck pupil Porphyry:

> [Plotinus] was wholly concerned with thought...Even if he was talking to someone, engaged in continuous conversation, he kept to his train of thought...In this way he was present at once to himself and to others, and he never relaxed his self-turned attention except in sleep: even sleep he reduced by taking very little food, often not even a piece of bread, and by his continuous turning in contemplation to his intellect.[7]

Hannah Arendt is trenchant on the tension between the solitary and the relational – or, as she terms it, between sovereignty and plurality:

> No man can be sovereign because not one man, but men, inhabit the earth – and not, as the tradition since Plato holds, because of man's limited strength, which makes him depend upon the help of others. All the recommendations the tradition has to offer to overcome the condition of non-sovereignty and win an untouchable integrity of the human person amount to a compensation for the intrinsic "weakness" of plurality. Yet, if these recommendations were followed and this attempt to overcome the consequences of plurality were successful, the result would be not so much sovereign domination of one's self as arbitrary domination of all others... (*Human Condition*, 234)[8]

Championing the "condition of non-sovereignty" returns us to the question of laughter and agency. When laughter arises, what is its relation to the person who laughs? Who is actually doing the laughing? "Laughter has God made me," Sarah exclaims. She herself vanishes as an agent in this consuming laughter. She is not doing the laughing; in some way, laughter is laughing her.

This seems to me to be true every time that we laugh in helpless delight: that we do not laugh, we are being laughed. The instability of laughter permeates our very selves. Arendt, in the passage quoted above, talks about the way in which the sovereignty of the individual is permanently challenged and limited by plurality, the fact that the individual is one among many. Laughter, in an odd way, takes plurality for granted by ignoring it; and yet laughter is infectious: one person, seeing another laugh, will often be compelled to join in. The passive voice is revealing: "be compelled" by what? Often, by the laughter itself. We do not need to have heard the joke, to have seen the clowning, to start to laugh. Once again, the "sovereignty of the individual" is challenged, for the individual is overcome by the laughter.

DOI: 10.1057/9781137370914

Arendt again:

> In view of human reality and its phenomenal evidence, it is…as spurious to deny human freedom to act because the actor never remains the master of his acts as it is to maintain that human sovereignty is possible because of the incontestable fact of human freedom. The question which then arises is whether our notion that freedom and non-sovereignty are mutually exclusive is not defeated by reality, or to put it another way, whether the capacity for action does not harbor within itself certain potentialities which enable it to survive the disabilities of non-sovereignty. (*Human Condition*, 235–6)

Giorgio Agamben adds to these "potentialities" the notion of "impotentiality": if human freedom is defined by the capacity – the potential – to act in certain ways, it is also defined by the capacity *not* to act in certain ways. To attain the fullest possible sense of human freedom, we need the fullest possible sense of both positive and negative potential. Agamben is building on Aristotle, *Metaphysics* Theta: "all potentiality (*dynamis*) is impotentiality (*adynamia*) of the same and with respect to the same."[9] From this, Agamben concludes that, "to be free is…*to be capable of one's own impotentiality*"; and "*The greatness of human potentiality is measured by the abyss of human impotentiality.*"[10]

Laughter shows the way in which our status as individuals is yet always, inevitably, predicated on our status *among* individuals: it shows the porous boundaries between singularity and plurality. It also shows that the individual, with her or his potential for action or not to act, is under some circumstances an illusory notion: when dissolved into laughter, embraced by its essential instability, then individuation becomes, briefly, meaningless.

There is no sovereign subject in laughter; there is no agency in laughter. Willed laughter is not laughter at all.

It emerges, then, that when I talk here about "specificity," it is not the specificity of the individual to which I am adverting – for all that, under other circumstances, I consider the specificity of the individual epistemologically significant – but the specificity of an instance of laughter. It is this narrowing of the application of specificity to laughter alone that shows more clearly than anything else the instability that *is* laughter.

The essential instability of laughter (the oxymoron is intentional) has been brilliantly placed at the heart of a new theory of comedy by Alenka Zupančič, *The Odd One In*. She argues that "comic subjectivity proper does not reside in the subject making the comedy, nor in the subjects or egos that appear in it, but in…incessant and irresistible, all-consuming movement. Comic subjectivity is *the very movement* of comedy" (3). The emphasis here is mine: Zupančič's efforts to think *through* movement are a truly novel contribution. Her theory is deeply inflected by Lacan and Zižek; it builds on Freud to account for the eruption – the "release" – of laughter; but it reads first and foremost as a creative re-working of Bergson. While she recognizes the limits of Bergson's "aprioristic and rather abstract" dualism (114) – his description of laughter, or comic effect, as caused by "the mechanical encrusted upon the living," *du mécanique plaqué sur du vivant*[11] – she nonetheless uses it to build her theory of the comic: "the mechanical element in the comic is not simply one of its two sides or compounds, but *the very relationship between the two*" (118, my emphasis again). She later relates this to the "dimension of precariousness and fundamental uncertainty in our very world that gets articulated and becomes manifest in every joke" (143). The work goes on to explore the ethical effect of unmasking this point of juncture, what Zupančič calls the *articulation*: if this can be accomplished, for a moment (she argues) we dislodge the mastery of the Master-Signifier, $S_1$, over the object $a$ (198) – that is, the "mastery" of words over things. In the end, she returns specifically to comedy: "the function and operation of the copula" is central to comedy – the copula being now not Bergson's, between the mechanical and the living, but that between "life and the signifier" (213–14); and this places comedy at "the most sensitive and precarious point of [the social] fabric, the point where it is being generated and regenerated, torn apart and fused together, solidified or transformed" (216). Zupančič grapples with how comedy functions in the dynamic interaction of the body with meaning – or meaninglessness; of the physical with the metaphysical. She puts that instant of spilling over between apparently incommensurable categories at the heart of her notion of comedy.

What has this to do with the laughter of Sarah? Zupančič's theory addresses comedy, not, strictly speaking, laughter; she takes it for granted that the pleasure engendered in the audience by perceiving the *articulation* will give rise to laughter, without discussing the properties of the laughter itself. Sarah is not laughing at a joke – unless we take God's bestowal of the impossible child to be an impossibly outsize joke (which is perhaps not such an inappropriate way to interpret it). But Zupančič draws our attention to the fundamental instabilities that accompany laughter: instabilities of meaning, of experience, of personal

DOI: 10.1057/9781137370914

identity. She characterizes human beings themselves not as composed of dualities – body and mind, or "the biological and the symbolic" – but as being "so many points where the difference between the two elements [of body and mind], as well as the two elements themselves as defined by this difference, are generated, and where the relationship between the two dimensions thus generated is being constantly negotiated" (214). And beyond even this notion of the human being, it is critical that Zupančič locates the comic moment, the moment that engenders laughter, in movement itself. Laughter is not static, and we do not laugh at something immobile. Laughter is all about motion, slippage, process: it embraces, and re-enacts, the instability of meaning.

Clearly, instability is difficult to talk or write about, reluctant to be pinned down – taking "reluctant" in its most literal sense, "struggling against" fixity. Yet Zupančič's theory of comedy gives us an attempt to place movement, or *articulation*, at the heart of a theory; and this is helpful for developing the notion of instability.

Laughter is an appropriate, indeed unavoidable, response to aspects of being in the world: it delightfully conquers and dissolves the laugher. We have seen in both Zupančič and Beauvoir that laughter is, in complicated but inevitable ways, linked with meaning: for Zupančič, it exposes the disjuncture between master-signifier and object, and hence dislocates meaning; for Beauvoir, the very way in which laughter encapsulates ambiguity gives meaning to the ambiguities of the world. In our passage from Augustine's letter to Paulinus of Nola, Augustine links laughter not just with the "bodily delights" in which his congregation is still lamentably enmeshed, but with meaninglessness, "empty speech" (*loqui vana*, literally "speaking vain things"). And yet it is the empty speech, with all that it actually contains of the world, that makes him laugh. The speech is (Augustine tries to convince himself) morally empty – but it is not contentless. Augustine struggles against the laughter engendered by this empty speech.

Jerome, of all people, inadvertently provides support for the powerful instability of laughter. In the course of his *Commentary on Ecclesiastes*, he is glossing the verse, "Anger is better than laughter, because in a sorrowful countenance the heart will be corrected" (Eccl. 7:3). Jerome writes crisply, "Laughter dissolves the mind, anger corrects and improves it" (*risus dissolvit mentem, ira corripit et emendat*). Dissolving the mind is, needless to say, not a good thing for Jerome. The contrast with *emendare* is revealing. Literally, the verb is compiled from *e*, "out," and *mendum*,

DOI: 10.1057/9781137370914

"fault": it means to remove faults. To divide, to separate, to discriminate: all these are possible extensions of its meaning. This is, for Jerome, the object of the best endeavors and the best teachers: to separate the good from the bad, to pare away foolishness, to divide – and to make the chastened pupil realize his error. Jerome's commentary on the very next passage, "the heart of the wise is in the house of grieving and the heart of the foolish in the house of delight," makes this clear:

> Paul says that he grieves over those who don't wish to repent after their various sins. So the heart of the wise goes to the house of the sort of man who corrects himself when he fails, so as to lead to tears…and not to the house of delight, where the teacher (*doctor*) fawns and deceives, and seeks not the conversion of his hearers, but applause and praise. (*Comm. in Eccl.* 7.5)

Laughter and delight lead, as in Augustine, to "empty speech," dissolution of proper distinctions, dissolution of the mind.

Dissolution is, of course, unacceptable in this worldview. And yet the constant anxiety to divide and separate – found not just in Jerome, but everywhere in the patristic sources and in the rich tradition that derives from them[12] – argues tacitly for the opposite position: that instead of this tendency toward division and subdivision, there is in human life a strong centripetal force, a tendency for the apparently incompatible or incommensurable to remain in ever-labile interrelation. What if laughter does dissolve the mind – and that dissolution is somehow expressive of the way things are? What if there is not the sharp division that Augustine struggles to draw between laughter in life and suitable weeping or mortification? What if the failure of that division is not just the way things are, but is even a good thing? For it is in this dissolution that a sense of possibility emerges: the essential lability of laughter may paradoxically be a creative "undoing," not a destructive one.

Judith Butler has written, as a clarion call, "Let's face it. We're undone by each other. And if we're not, we're missing something" (*Undoing Gender,* 19). She too is thinking here about the relation of the one to the many, of the way in which, "constituted as a social phenomenon in the public sphere, my body is and is not mine" (21). She introduces the notion of a "grievable life" as a life in the process of being recognized as truly human: this is clearly very different from the reflexivity of Jerome's "sort of man who corrects himself when he fails, so as to lead to tears." Butler writes, "We can say grief contains within it the possibility of apprehending the fundamental sociality of embodied life, the ways in which we are

DOI: 10.1057/9781137370914

from the start, and by virtue of being a bodily being, already given over, beyond ourselves, implicated in lives that are not our own" (22).

Can this notion apply to laughter too? Certainly, laughter "contains within it the possibility of apprehending the fundamental sociality of embodied life." The difference between the semantic operation of grief and laughter becomes immediately apparent, however, if we try a direct replacement of terms. A "grievable life" carries with it its own weight and significance. Butler is trying to expand the sphere of grievable lives – in other words, of lives considered weighty and significant; the notion that grief might confer significance is not in contention. But a "laughable life", in common parlance, can only mean "a life which may be laughed *at*." To observe that a life was laughable would not be kind or generous. Yet a life that has been receptive to laughter, that is capable of laughter, that may at any moment dissolve in laughter: can that too be a "laughable life"? Can we nudge the meaning of "laughable" away from derision and toward delight?

How well this shows that, when we are talking about laughter, we are trapped in a set of semantic and syntactic relations that do not suit it – or rather, that suit only a small part of its capacious range. Our own limitations and suspicions have restricted our use of language. We cannot talk about instability or lability or even ambiguity in a way that truly captures what we mean. Agamben tries to get the sense of unlimited possibility by thinking through the notion of "impotentiality," but even that founders on the limitations of language. To assign a name – laughter – to something essentially unstable is already, anomalously, to fix it in place. A laughter that laughs us, in which we are subsumed, in which the conventional organizing structures of language are defied: this is what we shall explore in the subsequent chapter.

So here we are, allowing the possibility that "empty speech" might be valuable, willingly capitulating in the struggle against laughter, allowing ourselves to be conquered and dissolved – to see what happens next.

# Notes

1   Basil of Caesarea, *Regulae Fusius Tractatae* 17, PG 31 cols. 889–1052.
2   I made this observation in a review of Halliwell: *Bryn Mawr Classical Review* 2009.09.69 (http://bmcr.brynmawr.edu/2009/2009-09-69.html).
3   Cf. Pin-Fat: "ever-present conditions of failure are what make ethico-political contestation and engagement possible," *Universality, Ethics and International*

DOI: 10.1057/9781137370914

*Relations: A grammatical reading* (London and New York: Routledge, 2010), 122.

4  See *conf.* 4.4, "I had become a great question to myself" (*factus eram ipse mihi magna quaestio*), effectively repeated at *conf.* 10.33, and C. Mathewes' important article, "The Liberation of Questioning in Augustine's *Confessions*", *Journal of the American Academy of Religion* 30 (2002), 539–60.

5  "In the earthly domain all glorification of the earth is true as soon as it is realized" – in contrast, once again, to Plato, where "art is mystification because there is the heaven of ideas," Beauvoir, S. de, *The Ethics of Ambiguity* tr. B. Frechtman (New York: Philosophical Library, 1948), 157.

6  Note too Bersani, L. "Sociality and Sexuality," *Critical Inquiry* 26 (2000), 641–56, in which he begins to construct a "genealogy of the relational" through a reading of Plato's *Symposium*.

7  Porphyry, *On the Life of Plotinus* tr. A. H. Armstrong, Loeb Classical Library (Cambridge, MA: Harvard University Press, 1966), 8. Having noted this passage, I should add that, notwithstanding the theoretical preoccupations of Porphyry, Plotinus himself did not gloss over the complexities and tensions of the relationship between being in the body and aspiring to spiritual transcendence of the body, as is shown especially by his two marvellous *Enneads* "On difficulties about the soul": see *Enneads* IV tr. A. H. Armstrong, Loeb Classical Library (Cambridge, MA: Harvard University Press, 1984), 4.3 and 4.4.

8  Invocation of "the tradition" notwithstanding, note Cicero's observation at *Rep.* 1.39: humans come together in civic organization not because of *imbecillitas*, weakness, but because of a *naturalis* tendency to congregate.

9  Aristotle, *Metaphysics* IX: 1046a.30–1 ed. W. Jaeger (Oxford: Clarendon Press, 1957).

10  *Potentialities* (Stanford CA: Stanford University Press, 2000), 183, 182; Agamben's emphasis.

11  Bergson, H. *Le Rire: essai sur la signification du comique* (Paris: Quadrige/PUF, 1940; first published 1900), 29.

12  For example, look at the energy with which another father of the church, Ambrose, resists the notion of the "wrong" type of laughter: when Noah gets drunk, and his son Ham laughs at the nakedness of his father, Ambrose says, "The person who laughed at his father was the one who was truly drunk [not Noah]. ... he did not see what he thought he was seeing; for the person who cannot see his own father has a profound blindness within him" (*De Noe* ed. Schenkl, CSEL 32, 1 (Vienna 1897), 31, 118). The dialectic of "wise" and "foolish" alone (and Ham in this story is of course "foolish," *insipiens*) shows how firmly these divisions are enforced.

DOI: 10.1057/9781137370914

# 6

# "Empty Speech": Laughter and Language

**Abstract:** *This chapter addresses the paradox of laughter and communication, posing the question: if laughter is radically unstable, how can it relate to language? Laughter clearly is a mode of communication; its textual representation is quite consistent across languages; and yet it cannot be reproduced or paraphrased. Using especially Adriana Cavarero and Hélène Cixous, I show that the laughter of delight, though it has meaning, is irreducibly itself, unique and uncapturable. It is epistemologically inappropriate, and cannot be contained in conventional modes of interpretation: the moment of laughter can only be expressed as itself.*

Conybeare, Catherine. *The Laughter of Sarah: Biblical Exegesis, Feminist Theory, and the Concept of Delight.*
New York: Palgrave Macmillan, 2013.
DOI: 10.1057/9781137370914.

DOI: 10.1057/9781137370914

What are the consequences of dissolution through laughter? If laughter is radically unstable, how can it relate to language, which offers some form of fixity? In laughter, what possibilities remain for representation?

We can talk *about* laughter – this is clear already in the biblical account of Sarah's laughter – but in fundamental ways it resists representation. We can allude to laughter, but we cannot recreate it in the way in which we can re-speak words.

It is not that we cannot gesture toward the representation of laughter: indeed, these gestures are remarkably consistent across languages. From English "ha ha ha" to Greek *cha cha cha*[1] (the *ch* is guttural) to Arabic *qahqaha*,[2] it is clearly the same sound that is being mimicked – the same sound that is being heard across cultures and times. This gives the illusion of representation: of in some way producing the sound of laughter. But equally clear is the fact that reading such a sound off the page, however urgent the attempt at mimesis, is very different from actually laughing. We can refer to laughter, but we cannot reproduce it.

Why is this so different from words? Are not words always divorced from the things they represent? Yes; and they are interwoven and inter-related to create a world of meaning. Different instances of laughter bear no such relationship to each other. There is no clear relationship between a burst of laughter and a "thing" or event that has prompted it. Nor are instances of laughter interwoven and interrelated. They are unique and indivisible, and mimic nothing in the perceptible world. If we consider laughter – the event itself, not the word "laughter" – as a sign (for it does, in some way, have meaning), then this is an instance in which *signum* really is the same as *res*.[3]

In thinking about the uniqueness of laughter, and its resistance to representation, we have a precursor in Adriana Cavarero's philosophical reflections on the nature of the voice.[4] Her over-arching purpose is to critique the philosophical obsession with the disembodied metaphysical *logos*, "word," at the expense of real words, spoken by individuals – and hence, of "voice." She "concentrates on the vocal and ignores the seman-tic" (2), in opposition to what she dubs "traditional philosophy" – which, for Cavarero, is philosophy grounded in the Platonic tradition. Many years before her work on voice, indeed, Cavarero captured this opposi-tion instead through the story of the laughter of the Thracian servant girl, when she sees the philosopher Thales, lost in thought, falling into a well. The unnamed Thracian servant laughs not just at the absurdity of the sight before her:

DOI: 10.1057/9781137370914

She is laughing at the foundational falsehood that the language of the West inherited from philosophy. Here the concept of verisimilitude (that which simulates the true) is generated from the dematerialization of what constitutes truth. This disavowal of reality penetrates everything, takes root, grows, and covers things up. Thus the world of life does not disappear but lies hidden.[5]

So in Cavarero's work on voice, her principal objective is to unveil the "world of life": in effect, to be seduced by the vital instead of the metaphysical.[6] In giving significance to the occluded notion of "voice" – the sound of words uttered, their tone, their pace, the utterly individual cast of each person's expression of sound – she is defiantly giving significance to the notion of uniqueness, which, as she says, tends to be dismissed as "epistemologically inappropriate" (9).

Cavarero illustrates the uniqueness of voice with a story about Isaac – though she does not adduce the meaning of his name. When Isaac is old and blind (Genesis 27), his younger son Jacob comes to him and tricks Isaac into blessing Jacob as if he were the older son, Esau. Isaac asks to touch Jacob – and touches the goat pelt with which Jacob has simulated his brother's hairy skin. Isaac trusts the touching and believes that Jacob is Esau. And yet, he has doubted the voice – or rather, he has identified it correctly, but does not trust his own instinct: "The voice is the voice of Jacob and the hands are Esau's hands" (Gen. 27:22, Alter's translation). Despite the individuality of the voice, the sense impression imparted by touch wins out. From the story of Isaac wilfully mistaking Jacob for Esau, Cavarero builds an account of the way in which sight (not in fact touch[7]) has become the dominant metaphor in Western philosophy, at the expense of sound/voice: we are all supposed to be striving for the perfect contemplative vision, *theoria*, which marks union with The One (round 173). Sound, it seems, falls low in the sensory hierarchy – some way below sight, contemplation, *theoria*, that highest of functions, attending to which Thales falls down his well. The incongruous juxtaposition of Jacob's voice and Esau's hairy hands might have seemed a joke, had the two things been given equivalent epistemic status; but the laughter of "he-will-laugh" cannot be realized, for despite his blindness Isaac has not yet learned to value sound.

We might add – as Cavarero does not – that Isaac fails to value sound in spite of its revelatory nature in his own earlier story. This moment of revelation occurs in the only extended episode in the Hebrew scriptures in which Isaac takes an active role. He has taken refuge from a famine with the king of the Philistines, Abimelech, in Gerar. In fear that the

DOI: 10.1057/9781137370914

Philistines will kill him to take his wife, Rebekah, he claims that she is his sister.

> And it happened, as his time there drew on, that Abimelech king of the Philistines looked out the window and saw – and there was Isaac playing with Rebekah his wife. And Abimelech summoned Isaac and he said, "Why, look, she is your wife, and how could you say, 'She is my sister'?" (Gen. 26:8–9)

The "sound" is not immediately apparent in the English translation; but the verb for "playing" is identical to the one for "laughing," whose root is embedded in Isaac's own name.[8] Here, clearly, it has sexual overtones – such that Abimelech can immediately detect the nature of the relationship between the two: it is the sound of the flirtatious, intimate laughter that has alerted him to the truth.

The laughter here is an example of what Cavarero means by "voice": something irreducibly corporeal, individual, unmistakeable. While Cavarero's overall philosophical project deeply undergirds my own, here I want to take her observations specifically about the voice and use them to build our notions of laughter.

As Cavarero warms to her theme, she writes, "The voice first of all signifies itself, nothing other than the relationality of the vocalic, which is already implicit in the first invoking cry of the infant" (169).[9] Augustine noticed this too – but the voice is not the only characteristic on which his perceptive account of infancy dwells. His tale of his own birth in the *Confessions* actually begins with the delights of suckling: "the consolations of human milk received me" (*conf.* 1.6.7).[10] This is then yoked together with three other activities:

> at that time I knew how to suckle and to give way to delight (*acquiescere delectationibus*), and to weep at physical discomfort, nothing more. Afterwards, I also began to laugh (*ridere*), first while asleep, then awake. (*conf.* 1.6.7–8)

(You will remember that Latin uses the same verb to express both laughter and smiling: that indeterminacy well suits the infant's first range of expression.) Each of these activities – the delightful suckling, "giv[ing] way to delight," the weeping, and the laughter – precedes both will and signification, as Augustine makes clear a couple of sentences later:

> and little by little I began to sense where I was, and I wanted to indicate my desires (*voluntates*) to those through whom they might be satisfied…and

DOI: 10.1057/9781137370914

> so I flung around my limbs and cries (*voces* – literally, "voices"), [making] signs – what few I could, and what sort I could – resembling my desires: but they weren't really similar. (*conf.* 1.6.8)

Will (*voluntas*) and signification are indissolubly bound together: they also require a developing sense of one's place in the world. But the suckling and delight, weeping and laughter, do not depend on a sense of place: each "signifies itself." If we may expand Augustine's account of lactation to include an audible aspect (as he does not), the happy grunts and snufflings of a baby at the breast "giv[ing] way to delight," then we can see how both suckling and weeping convey Cavarero's "relationality of the vocalic."

But the laughter is different. Also preceding signification, here it does not even express relationality. It occurs first in sleep (Augustine has observed well; so it does[11]): to whom or what, then, does it relate? Subsequently laughter emerges while awake, but again, it is not essentially relational. The succinctness of Augustine's formulation expresses this well: *post et ridere coepi, dormiens primo, deinde vigilans* ("afterwards, I also began to laugh, first while asleep, then awake"). There are no grammatical objects, direct or indirect, in this sentence; four of its eight words are verb-forms, three are adverbs, one is a conjunction with adverbial force (*et*). Laughter may come to express relationality, but it is not in itself about relationality. It is sufficient to itself; it is not willed, it signifies nothing but itself.

Cavarero observes subsequently of the infant exchange of sounds with the mother that this is not "dialogue" but "a cadence of demand and response" (170). Although laughter reflects the uniqueness, the irreproducibility of voice, here again we can see that not all she has to say about voice will apply to laughter: responsive it may be, demanding it is not. The social dynamics of laughter are not sequentially or hierarchically organized in the way invoked by "demand and response." In her marvellous meditation on motherhood, *Stabat Mater*, Julia Kristeva wrote,

> motherhood destines us to a demented *jouissance* that is answered, by chance, by the nursling's laughter...What connection is there between it and myself? No connection, except for that overflowing laughter where one senses the collapse of some ringing, subtle, fluid identity...[12]

The only response presupposed by laughter – the laughter of delight which we are considering – is laughter itself.

DOI: 10.1057/9781137370914

Looking back once more at the *post et ridere coepi* passage, we see that Augustine – wittingly or otherwise – has arranged the first activities of the infant in two contrasting pairs. Suckling and weeping express in their different ways urgent, reflexive needs: the need to eat, the need to be relieved of pain or discomfort. While strictly involuntary (in Augustine's account, at any rate), they are in a quite straightforward sense relational; they call on another person to respond to those needs. Laughter and the indeterminate "giv[ing] way to delight" are relational in a very different sense. They may invoke or create a relationship, but they do not *require* one. Even a baby can laugh, can be delighted, all by itself.[13] Laughter draws our attention to the permeability of the self, and – as we have seen – to the non-sovereign subject; but it does not need relationality.

Cavarero also writes that speech is the "essential destination" of the voice (12), but she protests against the notion that this is somehow the summation of the voice: "the sphere of the voice is constitutively broader than that of speech: it exceeds it" (13). And she adds, "To reduce this excess to mere meaninglessness ... is one of the chief vices of logocentrism." Thinking in these terms, what might be the "essential destination" for laughter? And what the "excess" that precedes and spills beyond that destination? The question immediately shows the difference of laughter from voice. For though it is similarly unique, in occasion and utterance, it neither precedes nor exceeds anything, and the only way we can conceive of its "essential destination" is reflexively. The destination of laughter is laughter itself. It cannot be expressed otherwise without becoming, not constrained and diminished, as voice is constrained into language, but simply other than itself.

There is much in Cavarero's thinking that can be related to laughter, but we have to tread carefully. Cavarero's focus on voice leads her to observe that sounds are dynamic events, and transitory by nature: she adds that they are characterized by "not being, but becoming" (37). We saw in our discussion of the volatility of laughter, and particularly of Zupančič's thought, something of its dynamic nature. Laughter is the perfect expression of the dynamic and the transitory; for what is the "essence" of laughter – "essence" derived from the later Latin word *essentia*, meaning "being" – if not (ironically) volatility, instability, the very opposite of the fixity with which true "being" is traditionally associated? And yet, it is not about "becoming" as such; for becoming relates to an end point, to something which the thing in process will eventually

DOI: 10.1057/9781137370914

become, whereas the essence of laughter *is* the process. Volatility is at the heart of laughter.

To distinguish between "becoming" and the notion of essential volatility or dynamism, we may read an early part of the Abraham and Sarah story – the changing of their names – in two different ways. The sound of laughter is present in the story of Abraham and Sarah almost from the beginning. In our first reading, it is emblematic of the act of becoming. God says to Abraham,

> "As for Me, this is My covenant with you: you shall be father to a multitude of nations. And no longer shall your name be called Abram but your name shall be Abraham, for I have made you father to a multitude of nations. ..."
> And God said to Abraham, "Sarai your wife shall no longer call her name Sarai, for Sarah is her name." (Gen. 17:4–5 and 15)

Neither of the changes of name really changes the name's meaning (for all that Philo and the Christian exegetes try to make it so). In each case, all that has happened is that one extra letter of the Hebrew alphabet – *Hē*, pronounced *"ha"* – has been inserted. In other words, we might say that it is the *ha* of laughter that enlivens God's new covenant with Abraham.[14] Yet a reading in terms of "becoming" will emphasize what the laughter turns into, for the notion of "becoming" presumes an end point: once the laughter in the name change is taken as in some way predicting or guaranteeing God's covenant, we return to the sort of blatant teleological reading that we explored in chapter 2.[15]

Alternatively, in our second reading, we might simply relate the *ha* of the new names to the creative outward gasp that is God's breath or spirit, the *ruah*, to which Cavarero devotes a rhapsodic passage early in her book: "The term *ruah* indicates above all breath – the living breath of God breathed into the mouth of Adam – or, rather, that same divine breath that exhales into the chaos before naming the elements that flow from his breath" (20). For, as I wrote at the end of chapter 3, the laughter of Sarah, the laughter of delight, simply is.

In Irigaray's *The Way of Love* – in which like Cavarero she is much preoccupied with voice, with sound, and with reciprocity (there is a rhapsodic passage on Air which mirrors that of Cavarero on breath[16]) – she discusses how to express this sort of dynamism without a *telos*, an end point. Irigaray's concern is with "speaking between subjects," not laughing between subjects, but she has much to say that is relevant here. Recall Augustine's sentence: *post et ridere coepi, dormiens primo, deinde*

DOI: 10.1057/9781137370914

*vigilans.* Translated literally, word for word and with the words in the same order, this reads: "Afterwards also to laugh [I] began, sleeping initially, then waking." There is no subject expressed, bar that implicit in the verb *coepi.* The other three verbs are an infinitive, *ridere*, and two participles, *dormiens* and *vigilans.* Irigaray would approve:

> The verb will perhaps be more effective than the substantive for laying out traces, sketching perspectives, outlining horizons. The verb of which the act will be sometimes assumed by a subject, sometimes left in an infinitive form... The verb of which the tense can be modulated: recalling a past, opening a future, remaining in the present or trying to arrive in it, to dwell in it, and which serves to build bridges between different moments, inside a single subjectivity or between two subjects. (59)

Meanwhile, "the substantive in a way immobilizes time. ... [It] represents a kind of ideal in designating, an idea of the thing thanks to the name attributed to it" (62–3). Perhaps we are beginning to get at the ways in which the naming of laughter fails us. Yes, grammatically laughter is a noun; but what the noun "laughter" represents is the very opposite of "immobiliz[ed] time."[17] It is time as fluid, immediate, shifting.

Latin, Greek, and – in a different way – Hebrew are all more resistant to this immobilization of time than English: far more can be conveyed with a verb alone. And hence there is a dynamism in these languages and their modes of signification that English cannot express directly, and has to strain to paraphrase. The dynamism of these verb forms may approximate to the expression of laughter, but in the end it cannot begin to match it.

There is a further twist to Irigaray's argument that bears thinking about. She pleads against privileging verbs that take a direct object, and hence immediately, inherently propose a relation of dominance, a subject-object relation.[18] She attempts instead to formulate ideas around verbs and indirect objects, to express a subject-subject relation – hinted at above in her remark about building bridges "inside a single subjectivity or between two subjects." Her example – which she admits involves a "transformation of discourse" – is "I love to you," which she glosses as "I love to who you are, to what you do, without reducing you to an object of my love" (60). Greek or Latin might express this with an ethic dative, a concept sadly lacking in English: this is a word, usually a personal pronoun, in the dative case, which expresses a loose relationship to the verb as a thing aspecifically concerned or affected.[19] Pedantic translation

DOI: 10.1057/9781137370914

might capture the notion with something like "I love with reference to you" (it would be *amo tibi* in Latin).

It is easy to see how we might replace "love" with "laugh," for "to laugh" never has a direct object, only indirect ones. "Whoever hears will laugh with me"; "Whoever hears will laugh at me" – but they cannot laugh me. "Laughter has God made me" – complete in itself, not dominating or possessing or needing any object. The one exception to this rule we already saw when we were discussing the notion of agency in laughter. Laughter laughs itself, as well as the person laughing: it may be both subject and object of laughter.

Both Irigaray and Cavarero characterize their work as in part a recovery of the female subject or of female spheres of action – and diction. There is no inherent reason why women should more particularly own the sphere of "voice" (Cavarero) or of the "subject-subject" relationship (Irigaray[20]) – except (the argument goes) that they are forced into that position: into a creative circumvention of a discursive model that has long excluded them. Such coercion may be attributed to a longstanding tradition that has recently and cogently found expression in the work of Jacques Lacan. When Cavarero writes of the "sonorous, libidinal, and presemantic materiality of logos" and of the "division of logos into a purely feminine *phone* and a purely masculine *semantikon*" (102, 107), it is Lacan, above all, who is hovering in the background.

For Lacan has argued that woman is always already excluded from meaning and language – from the *semantikon*, or the realm of the "symbolic." "There is woman only as excluded by the nature of things which is the nature of words, and it has to be said that if there is one thing they themselves are complaining about enough at the moment, it is well and truly that – only they don't know what they are saying, which is all the difference between them and me" (*Feminine Sexuality*, 144). Feminist scholars are understandably enraged by this sort of sentiment, although ultimately it is a claim about epistemology – if "woman" is indeed "excluded by...the nature of words," then in a strict epistemological sense, she cannot "know" what she is saying. Lacan's position is largely descriptive, not prescriptive. Whether the description is right or not is another question: but it is hard to argue with a claim like "There is no such thing as *The* woman, where the definite article stands for the universal" (144 again) (hence Lacan's insistence on writing ~~The~~ *woman*), even if one does not wish to go on to argue that the consequence is woman's exclusion from language.[21]

DOI: 10.1057/9781137370914

It is in this context that Julia Kristeva developed her notion of the semiotic to enrich Lacan's symbolic, his disembodied account of language. The disembodied subject (or "transcendental ego") seems to be the lovechild of linguistics and philosophy. Kristeva insisted instead that language be situated in the bodies that produce it. Language, for Kristeva, is no longer merely associated with the "symbolic order" of syntax, rationality, logical thought, with which the child is instilled in the name of the father at the oedipal stage of development, the stage of coming into language; the pre-oedipal semiotic realm also makes itself heard, through tone of voice, rhythm of speech, and various forms of syntactic rupture, and this anchors speech firmly in the body of the speaker and in the moment of speaking.[22] Kristeva resists consideration of the word separate from the time and manner of its utterance: both semiotic and symbolic modes are simultaneously present in speech, though in terms of infant development ("infant" meaning literally *in-fans*, "not-speaking") the semiotic precedes the symbolic. As Cavarero sums up: "The vocalic practice of the semiotic – in which the child is immersed, in the free play of the articulation and differentiation of sounds, tones, and rhythms – ends up being indispensable to the phonematic system of language. Language, in short, exploits, reduces, and regulates the marvelous exercises of the infantile voice" (*For More than One Voice*, 133).

Augustine mapped the importance of the semiotic realm sixteen hundred years ago, in a passage of the *Confessions* that – in the midst of that much-read work – has largely eluded commentary.

> For a while as an infant I certainly knew no Latin, and yet by paying attention I learned without fear and torture at all, between the crooning of nurses and the jokes of those who smiled on me and the laughter of playmates (*inter... blandimenta nutricum et ioca adridentium et laetitias adludentium*). I learnt Latin without any pressure of punishment from others, since my heart urged me to produce its own thoughts... [and I could not have done so] had I not learnt some words, not from people teaching me but from people talking to me, in whose ears I too gave birth to whatever I felt. (*conf.* 1.14.23)

"Between the crooning of nurses and the jokes of those who smiled on me and the laughter of playmates": how perfectly Augustine captures here a pre-oedipal stage of language acquisition which is all about embodied utterance of sounds – not necessarily words. Crooning, joking, laughter: eventually (we do not know how eventually, because a part

DOI: 10.1057/9781137370914

of the passage seems to be missing – hence the ellipsis) they are resolved into *aliqua verba*, "some words." Of the six Latin words that indicate the context in which Augustine comes into language, four evoke unequivocally laughter, play, and delight. Here is Kristeva's semiotic realm in its most joyful and reassuring form: language embodied, inarticulate, non-rational – and embedded in laughter.

In James O'Donnell's commentary on the *Confessions*, he remarks of the passage above, "There is no scripture in the paragraph ... The unscriptural text is at centre stage, infecting [*sic*] the narrative. The implicit assertion ... is that divine power goes even where the scriptural word is missing." Yes: this passage expresses beautifully the importance, not of the abstract, transcendent Word or *logos*, or even of the words that gesture toward it, but of the warmth of the embodied voice.

One more aspect of the passage bears mention here. The laughter and crooning are what bring Augustine into language "without fear and torture"; and they come from his nurses and playmates. Women – especially those of the underclasses – and children are not generally characterized as crucial to the formation of a speaking thinking being. But here they are.[23]

Having said that, it is a problem that once we start talking about the semiotic and the symbolic – or about voice and *logos* – we risk being caught in a creeping essentialism of gender. We hear this essentialism even – or perhaps especially – when writers attempt to circumvent it. Consider, for instance, Kristeva on Mallarmé: "Indifferent to language, enigmatic and feminine, this space underlying the written is rhythmic, unfettered, irreducible to its intelligible verbal translation; it is musical, anterior to judgement, but restrained by a single guarantee: syntax."[24] Or Lacan on mystics, men who recognize the female "*jouissance* which goes beyond" (*Feminine Sexuality*, 147).

For Lacan is deeply attached to the notion of female *jouissance* – the "*jouissance* proper to her" (145) – the moment of overflowing which (in Lacan's account) puts woman outside the "all" of the symbolic system, of language, and which ~~the~~ woman experiences as supplementary to the all, not complementary (for in that case "we'd fall right back into the all"). That this *jouissance* should be beyond language leads to the astonishing conclusion that it somehow exceeds the "all": such is the price of a determination to place the female outside language; and such is the reiteration of gender division even in a context that might move beyond it.

DOI: 10.1057/9781137370914

How to address this? On the one hand, in choosing to entitle my book *The Laughter of Sarah*, I am clearly in some way replicating the claim that women have privileged access to the realm of laughter. But while I am arguing that Sarah's laughter expresses something special and often overlooked, a particular eruptive delight, I do not wish to suggest that this laughter is unique to women. I turn for support to the marvellous essay of Hélène Cixous, a piece as eruptive and delightful and utterly individual as the laughter of Sarah itself: "The Laugh of the Medusa." First published in French in 1975, in English a year later, the essay is written from an explicitly and unabashedly female perspective.[25] But it does not, in the end, refuse the presence of others.

Cixous directly engages the legacy of Lacan and Freud – only to shrug it off:

> Their "symbolic" exists, it holds power – we, the sowers of disorder, know it only too well. But *we are in no way obliged to deposit our lives in their banks of lack*... (884; my emphasis)

She continues – still simultaneously engaging and dismissing Freud and Lacan:

> Too bad for them if they fall apart upon discovering that women aren't men, or that the mother doesn't have one. But isn't this fear convenient for them? Wouldn't the worst be, *isn't the worst*, in truth, *that women aren't castrated*, that they have only to stop listening to the Sirens (for the Sirens were men) for history to change its meaning? You only have to look at the Medusa straight on to see her. And she's not deadly. She's beautiful and she's laughing. (885; my emphasis again)

In the end, the motifs come together: "Castration? Let others toy with it. What's a desire originating from a lack? A pretty meager desire" (891). A woman, instead, "blazes *her* trail in the symbolic" (888, Cixous' emphasis); "she is dispersible, prodigious, stunning, desirous and capable of others, of the other woman that she will be, of the other woman she isn't, of him, of you" (890).

Listen to how Cixous, in this final swift outpouring, simply overturns the ever-iterated claims about Western selfhood. She does not argue against them: she simply states the opposite, and makes it sound both desirable and attainable. A woman is "dispersible": there goes the long-cherished integrity of the self! She is "prodigious": she exceeds bounds; she revels, not in improprieties, but in her own self-generated ideas of the proper; she casts as irrelevant the association of prodigies with

DOI: 10.1057/9781137370914

monsters, and embraces the abundance of prodigiousness. Above all, she is always already related to others, to their presents, to their futures, to their potentialities and their impotentialities. And those others may be anyone, of any gender.

The relationship with others, not "othered" as aliens, but simply expressing other possibilities, other presents and futures: this is what is lost in the notion of *jouissance* developed by Lacan – and for that matter, in very different vein, by Barthes in *Le Plaisir du Texte*. For *jouissance* means not just "pleasure" or "bliss," but "orgasm"; and the popular French notion of orgasm as a *petit mort*, a "little death," seems to be close behind both writers' interpretations of the word. In Barthes' words:

> The asocial character of *jouissance*: it is the abrupt loss of sociality, and yet there follows no recurrence to the subject (subjectivity), the person, solitude: *everything* is lost, integrally. Extremity of the clandestine, darkness of the cinema. (39 Eng.; 63 Fr. Slightly adapted)

Compare the *jouissance* of being outside the all; for what exceeds the "all" if not non-being, death?

And yet one might think that orgasm and laughter – the laughter of delight about which I have been talking all along – have much to do with each other. (Cixous would agree, I think: "The Laugh of the Medusa" is filled with orgasmic imagery.) This explosive delight, the spilling-over, the fleeting sense of endless possibility, the sense of boundaries breached – between body and mind, between self and other: can we not see this in both of them? Moreover, both laughter and orgasm – as events, not as words – collapse the distinction between *signum* and *res*: they *are* the thing that they express. Finally, each conveys meaning of sorts, but it is a meaning that cannot be expressed in words, or even paraphrased.[26]

Let us return to the relationship of laughter and language. Because of its peculiar – idiosyncratic – relationship to meaning and signification, laughter provides a way to interrogate both Lacan and Kristeva, and even to circumvent their sharply gendered divisions. There is a revealing moment in the seminar of Lacan which I have been quoting. "If the unconscious is indeed what I say it is, as being structured like a language…" (139). But what if the unconscious is *not* structured like a language? Or what if that language includes the unique communicative mode of laughter?

The possibility of re-thinking meaning through laughter, however incompletely, is irresistible. Laughter, after all, has meaning. We cannot

DOI: 10.1057/9781137370914

say that it does not make sense because clearly, on some level, it does: laughter is intelligible even if we can never exactly capture in words what it is communicating. So laughter is in some way a part of language, if an utterly idiosyncratic part. It is simultaneously *signum* and *res*. It is uncapturable as anything other than itself, in anything other than its own moment, but it gestures toward more than itself.

Suppose laughter were given credit as a communicative form of its own? And what if the unconscious were in fact all about this unique mode of expression – and not well expressed as "structured like a language" at all?

We are back with the "epistemologically inappropriate" uniqueness of laughter.[27] Laughter is beyond capture: it cannot be harnessed or re-directed or re-expressed. As a result, it exists for its own moment only.

# Notes

1  Neatly attested in one of the Greek magical papyri, in which God laughs the world into being: *P. Leiden* J395, tr. Betz, H. D. *The Greek Magical Papyri in Translation* vol. 1 (Chicago: Chicago University Press, 1992). Thanks to Radcliffe Edmonds for first telling me of this papyrus; it is briefly discussed in Halliwell, S. *Greek Laughter: A Study in Cultural Psychology from Homer to Early Christianity* (Cambridge: Cambridge University Press, 2008), 12–13.

2  See "Das Wortfeld 'Lachen' im Arabischen," in Ludwig Ammann, *Vorbild und Vernunft: Die Regelung von Lachen und Scherzen im mittelalterlichen Islam* (Hildesheim/Zürich/New York: G. Olms, 1993), 6–10.

3  This is to invoke Augustine's distinction between *signum* and *res*, representation and reality, as famously developed in *De Doctrina Christiana* ed./tr. R. P. H. Green (Oxford: Oxford University Press, 1995), 1.2.4–6; he develops this more subtly, and at greater length, in the earlier *De Magistro* ed. W. M. Green, CCL 29 (Turnhout 1970).

4  See Cavarero, A. *For More than One Voice. Towards a Philosophy of Vocal Expression* tr. P. A. Kottman (Stanford CA: Stanford University Press, 2005; first published in Italian, 2003).

5  "The Maidservant from Thrace," in eadem, *In Spite of Plato: a feminist rewriting of ancient philosophy* (New York and London: Routledge, 1995), 55.

6  Warnings against being "metaphysically seduced": Pin-Fat, V. *Universality, Ethics and International Relations: A Grammatical Reading* (London and New York: Routledge, 2010), 5 and *passim*, drawing on Wittgenstein. See also Braidotti's introduction to *In Spite of Plato*: "what Cavarero wishes to stress is

DOI: 10.1057/9781137370914

that the living being…precedes the inscription into the symbolic and thus is prior to its specific order" (xvii).

7    Cavarero does not develop this theme, but touch is, in fact, an anomalous sense, being the only one of the sense perceptions that has no sensory organ specifically associated with it: as Aristotle observes, "It is a problem whether touch is a single sense or a group of senses. It is also a problem, what is the organ of touch: is it or is it not the flesh?" Aristotle, *De Anima* II.11; 422$^b$.

8    The verb is related to the noun *tsehoq*, whose semantic range I discuss in chapter 1.

9    More specifically: "There is not yet any signified in this voice – no reference through the linguistic sign to the noetic *presence* of an absent object," *For More than One Voice*, 170.

10   Contrast Barthes' notion of "une succion sans objet," "ungratified sucking," to express a relation with an unsatisfactory, "prattling," text (*Le plaisir du texte* (Paris: Éditions du Seuil, 1973); *The Pleasure of the Text* tr. R. Miller (New York: Farrar, Straus and Giroux, 1975), 12 and 5 respectively.

11   Notwithstanding the deflationary note of O'Donnell in his commentary *ad loc.*: "Modern medicine ascribes the apparent smile of a sleeping newborn to flatulence"; contrast Sroufe, L. A. and E. Waters, "The Ontogenesis of Smiling and Laughter: A Perspective on the Organization of Development in Infancy", *Psychological Review* 83 (1976), 173–89.

12   Kristeva, J. "Stabat Mater" in eadem, *Histoires d'amour* (Paris: Éditions Denoël, 1983), 241–2. Kristeva also seems to be gesturing towards laughter's unrepresentability near the beginning of "Stabat Mater," when she writes, "Writing [words] down is an ordeal of discourse, like love. What is loving, for a woman, the same thing as writing. Laugh. Impossible" (226).

13   This reading relies on construing *acquiescere delectationibus*, "give way to delight," as a separate element, not a hendiadys with *sugere*, "suckle"; the urgent greedy need of a suckling baby is very different from its delighted burbling and belching after its hunger has been satisfied.

14   See also Parvalescu: "It is as if from now on Abraham and Sarah laugh a little when they say their own names," *Laughter: Notes on a Passion* (Cambridge, MA: MIT Press, 2010), 17.

15   Against this, compare the delightful inconsequentiality of Midrash on the removal from Sarah's name of *yod*, the letter transliterated in English as *i*: "The *yod* which the Lord took from Sarai soared aloft before God and protested: 'Sovereign of the Universe! Because I am the smallest of all letters, Thou has withdrawn me from the name of that righteous woman!'" *Midrash Rabbah: Genesis* tr. H. Freedman, 2 vols. (Oxford 1939), 47.1.

16   *The Way of Love* (London and New York: Continuum, 2002), 66–8. Irigaray and Cavarero do not, however, refer to each other's work; and the two

DOI: 10.1057/9781137370914

books were originally published almost simultaneously (2002 and 2003 respectively).

17　Compare Augustine *De Magistro* 5.14, on *est,* "it is," as a noun (based on a Latin version of 2 Cor. 1:19, *non erat in Christo est et non, sed est in illo erat*) – which ultimately demonstrates, not the fixity, but the dynamism of language.

18　Note Snediker, M. *Queer Optimism: Lyric Personhood and other Felicitous Persuasions* (Minneapolis, MN: University of Minnesota Press, 2008), 10 for a different way of re-thinking the subject-object relation around the "durability" of the object – "its own capacity for loving in spite of feeling damaged, or even repelled, by the subject" – again conflating language and bodies.

19　Given that I am sketching here an ethics of relationality, the "ethic dative" seems a particularly pertinent form.

20　Irigaray, L. *Way of Love,* 24: "Of course, speaking to many or speaking only to one does not presuppose the same relation to speech. In the first case, it must convey a meaning in some way closed, in which the speaking subject converses above all with their own self and with speech. No doubt this kind of meaning is the one that the masculine subject has always privileged./The feminine subject, on the other hand, takes an interest in the relation between two, in communication between two people." Page DuBois makes a similar point about pronoun usage in Sappho, without relating it to an essentialist gender position: see *Sappho is Burning* (Chicago: University of Chicago Press, 1995), 134–44.

21　"Lacan does provide some crucial elements for a description and explanation of the psychic components of women's oppression, although he himself does not acknowledge the structure of patriarchal oppression": Grosz, E. *Jacques Lacan: A Feminist Introduction* (London/New York: Routledge, 1990), 145. This book offers a clear discussion of Lacan's views, followed by an exposition and critique of feminist responses to him, especially those of Kristeva and Irigaray.

22　For a convenient excerpt, Kristeva, J. "The Semiotic and the Symbolic," in *The Women and Language Debate: A Sourcebook* ed. C. Roman, S. Juhasz, and C. Miller (New Brunswick, NJ: Rutgers University Press, 1994), 45–55; more extensively, Kristeva, J. *Revolution in Poetic Language* (New York: Columbia University Press, 1984; first published in French, 1974).

23　Note, however, Biddick's reclamation of the mother in early nineteenth-century models of language acquisition: "the mother sounded out words, syllable by syllable, and her children attended to the shaping of her lips and the sound of voice, and not to written letters, to learn their alphabet" (*The Typological Imaginary: Circumcision, Typology, History* (Philadelphia: University of Pennsylvania Press, 2003), 86). This is all part of Biddick's recovery of the "acoustical" properties overlooked or erased in Freud's thought – a project clearly pertinent to my own work here.

DOI: 10.1057/9781137370914

24  Kristeva, J. "The Semiotic and the Symbolic", 50.

25  Cixous, H. "The Laugh of the Medusa", *Signs* (Summer 1976), 875–93; revised version of 'Le rire de la méduse', *L'arc* (1975), 39–54.

26  Contrast Derrida's famous reading of Bataille on laughter: "Laughter alone exceeds dialectics and the dialectician: it bursts out *only on the basis of an absolute renunciation of meaning*" ("From restricted to general economy," in *Writing and Difference* tr. A. Bass (Chicago: University of Chicago Press, 1978; first published in French, 1967), 256; my emphasis).

27  "Epistemologically inappropriate": Cavarero, *For More than One Voice*, 9. Cf. Barthes, *Le plaisir du texte*: "Desire has an epistemic dignity, Pleasure does not." He relates the disjunction partly to social class in a way which recalls our discussion of laughter and power in chapter 3: "the 'populace' does not know Desire – only pleasures": Fr. 91–2; Eng. 57–8.

DOI: 10.1057/9781137370914

# 7
# A Time for Laughter

Abstract: *The final chapter explores the moment of laughter. Laughter does not merely challenge representation; it also challenges time. We cannot relate conventional notions of time to something that is of its nature volatile and sudden, and yet weirdly undifferentiated in its individual instances. This chapter shows how laughter makes its own time – in both senses of that ambiguous phrase – and prompts us to appreciate a radical openness in, and to, the world in the given moment. The chapter, and the book, end by showing how an appreciation of the laughter of delight upends a teleological reading of the world – hence the reluctance of biblical interpreters to "hear" it – and opens us instead to the delight of now.*

Conybeare, Catherine. *The Laughter of Sarah: Biblical Exegesis, Feminist Theory, and the Concept of Delight.* New York: Palgrave Macmillan, 2013. DOI: 10.1057/9781137370914.

Laughter exists for its own moment. Laughter does not merely challenge representation; it also challenges time. How can we relate conventional notions of time and duration to something which is of its nature volatile, sudden, and weirdly undifferentiated – for all that it is in some way intelligible?

It is fascinating that Henri Bergson, the great theorist of laughter, also thought deeply about time. Bergson tries to dissociate time from notions of space, and the possibilities of measurement and quantification that go along with them; but he does not, as far as I know, relate time to laughter.[1] Of time, he writes, "In the human soul there are only *processes*" (170); "the deep-seated conscious states have no relation to quantity, they are pure quality. ... The duration which they thus create is a duration whose moments do not constitute a numerical multiplicity" (173). We do not need to form a judgement on the existence of the soul to suggest that laughter, similarly, is "pure quality"; and that the moments of its duration "do not constitute a numerical multiplicity." Laughter extends in time, but it does not relate in a conventional way to time.

Zupančič's theory of the joke, which we discussed in chapter 5, is much preoccupied with how the dynamics of the joke relate to time: "the fundamental temporality of a joke [is] ... that of an *instant*."[2] It is that instant that catches the hearer and elicits laughter. But this, though pertinent, runs oblique to what we might be able to say of laughter: while the instantaneity of a joke relates to incipient laughter, it does not tell us about the quality of laughter itself. Parvalescu takes us further. Tucked into a footnote, she has a suggestive sentence: "Laughter is a challenge to narrative; a burst, it inhabits a dense 'now' that resists narrativization and spatialization."[3] The image of laughter as a "burst" – an *éclat de rire* – is a cogent one, and we shall return to it shortly. Meanwhile, if laughter resists narrative, it also resists explanation; and it takes time out of narrative. But can we attach meaning to the notion of time out of narrative?[4]

Compare Augustine, wrestling with the notion of time in Book 11 of the *Confessions*:

> And I acknowledge to you, Lord, that I still don't know what time is, and again I acknowledge to you, Lord, that I know that I am saying these things in time, and that I'm talking for a long time about time, and that that very "long time" isn't a "long time" except through the lapse of time. So how do I know this, when I don't know what time is? (*conf.* 11.25.32)

DOI: 10.1057/9781137370914

So think about it: the corporeal voice begins to sound, and it sounds, and it is still sounding, and look – it stops, and now there is silence, and that voice has passed and the voice exists no longer.... it could [be measured] when it was sounding, because then it was something which could be measured. But even then it was not stationary; it went and passed on. (*conf.* 11.27.34)[5]

"Even then it was not stationary." Think of Bergson: "In the human soul there are only processes." Augustine is thinking about time in terms of the human voice: its sound, and its passing. His starting point is that he knows *that* time is, he just doesn't know *what* time is. Ultimately, he expresses the passing of time through an account of syllabification in the singing of a hymn. Because one can count the syllables, because one has sufficient memory of them to mark them comparatively as short or long in duration, one can therefore achieve some sort of sense of the passing of time.[6]

Brian Stock, in his recent work on Augustine's dialogues, takes this one step further: Augustine "proposes that words are perceived in a sequence of sounds... and, with the aid of memory, they are given meaning. And at the moment when this meaning is created the passage of time appears momentarily to have been suspended." Augustine's aim is then "to move forward from narrative, which takes place in time, to a meditative state of mind, which is outside time."[7]

But what about laughter? If the relationship of voice to time is complicated, and indeed inexpressible without the mediation of memory, how much more so is the relationship of laughter to time? Laughter certainly has duration. But we cannot break it down into syllables – or any other constituent parts. And it cannot be mediated by memory. Unlike with speaking, we can remember that we laughed, but we cannot – as it were – remember *what* we laughed. Instantaneously prompted, laughter is utterly irrecuperable. It is not that laughter does not exist in time, it is that it has its own relationship to time.

In fact, laughter makes its own time. (The double meaning is intentional.) In the early Christian interpreters, much effort is expended on determining the right time – the *kairos* – for laughter. John Chrysostom inveighs in his fifteenth *Homily on the Letter to the Hebrews* (ch. 9) against laughter that is *para metron, to akairon* – "beyond measure, something untimely" – specifically, laughing in church, or at sacred things. He elaborates (self-defeatingly, one fears) with an outraged list of biblical episodes at which his congregation is prone to laugh: the list is punctuated with the repeated demand, *su de gelas;* "and you laugh?," and culminates with

DOI: 10.1057/9781137370914

"Do you not see how Sarah was honored? Do you not hear Christ saying, 'Woe to those who laugh, for they shall weep'?" Chrysostom allows that there are benign types of laughter, but concludes, "laughter has been placed in our soul so that sometimes the spirit should be relaxed, not so that it should be poured out (*diacheētai*)."[8]

Writing in more general terms, Clement of Alexandria points out that "whatever is natural to human beings ought not to be eliminated from them; instead, one ought to impose on those things a measure and an appropriate time (*kairon preponta*). Just because a human being is an animal capable of laughter (*gelastikon zōon*), it ought not to laugh at everything..." (*Paed.* II.5.46.1–2). This is an interesting set of moves: from not rooting out natural human qualities like laughter, to the need to impose moderation upon them, to the requirement "not to laugh at everything." But given that laughter is natural, why should it follow that laughter would be constant? (What, indeed, could constant laughter be?) Why the anxiety to enforce a *kairos prepōn* – a redundancy, for it means something like "an appropriate right time"? Clement takes for granted the tendency of laughter to break bounds, to spill over, to challenge the notion of the measured and fitting; and it makes him so anxious that this section, while acknowledging that laughter is natural, is all about delimitation and constraint.

But laughter, true ecstatic laughter, creates its own *kairos*. It is exactly about the pouring out, the bubbling over; and whatever time it occurs must be the right time. We see this with Sarah's exultant laughter at Isaac's birth. If we take the darker reading of the Hebrew – a fear that those hearing will laugh *at* her, not *with* her – we can see that this is, by many accounts, the wrong time to laugh. Sarah is drawing attention to the absurdity of an old, old woman giving birth, to the physical distastefulness of her old breasts suckling a baby – and yet she cannot help it. It is by definition the *kairos*, the right time, to laugh – for she laughs. The instant of laughter is irreducible to anything else or to any other considerations.

Back in chapter 1, we remarked on the range of interpretations of Sarah's laughter in the exegesis of the Qur'an (Surat al-Hud). The interpretation that gains most attention in Tabari's compilation of exegetical statements is that of menstruation – even if the closing remark is that "some of the linguists say: 'She laughed' is not attested in a trustworthy fashion with the meaning 'she menstruated.'" We originally construed menstruation as one of the elements that suggested "something

DOI: 10.1057/9781137370914

overflowing, exuberant, unbounded" about Sarah's laughter. But there is more. Clearly, this reading of laughter speaks to its situation in the body, and its relation to the embodied subject that laughs; but it also speaks to the ever-present timeliness of laughter, to the way laughter creates its own time. In the words of the second of Tabari's interpreters: "Mujahid said: She laughed – that is, she menstruated, when her age was some years more than ninety." The menstruation, clearly at the wrong time and yet – because God's command was to be fulfilled in the birth of Isaac – simultaneously at the right time, literalizes the way in which Sarah's laughter, too, is simultaneously at the wrong and right time. It is the *kairos* for menstruation; it is the *kairos* for laughter.

The *kairos* is the instant that dissolves ordinary patterns of language and meaning, that is only about itself. It has no measurable duration, and yet it exists. Whenever an outburst of laughter occurs, the laughter of delight, that is the *kairos*.

The *kairos* is the instant in which Zupančič locates the dynamics of the joke, in which Bergson detects "pure quality." It is the instant of *jouissance*, though not in the Lacanian reading. Listen instead to Jean-Luc Nancy: "Joy, *jouissance*, *to come*, have the sense of birth: the sense of the inexhaustible imminence of sense."[9] Note "imminence," not "immanence": the sense which is – always – about to be, not the sense which is within. Nancy brings this to his own reflections on laughter:

> Is it possible to be in the presence of laughter? Does laughter have a presence? That is: laughter itself, not the person laughing, nor the object of his/her laughter. Laughter always bursts – and loses itself in peals. As soon as it bursts out, it is lost to all appropriation, to all presentation.... [A]ll that is left of laughter is the absolute purity of its *burst*... Laughter is... neither a presence nor an absence. ("Laughter, Presence" in *Birth to Presence*: 368, 378, 383)[10]

Let us pause for a moment over the idea of laughter as a burst – an *éclat de rire*. There is certainly something very seductive about this notion. The suddenness of laughter lends itself to it. Remember Chrysostom narrating Sarah's exultation that suddenly, *athroon*, she has become a mother. It is not so much the process of becoming a mother that is sudden, in fact, but the laughter which marks it. But what do we really mean when we speak of a burst of laughter?

The suddenness of laughter, its *kairos*, is beyond question. And we are trying here to examine laughter from the midst of that *kairos*, rather

DOI: 10.1057/9781137370914

than in anticipation or retrojection. As Parvalescu observes, "one cannot say 'I laugh' in the present tense."[11] Well, we can, but clearly the statement cannot carry its literal meaning. But we are trying to think as if we could – or rather, as if we *are*, in the instant, saying "I laugh."[12]

In order for there to be a burst of laughter, something has to be ruptured. But what? The term seems to presuppose an ontological reality through which laughter will suddenly force itself. But laughter, too, is real; it has ontological status. Doesn't it? Or if it doesn't, what makes us think that it should?

One effect of this is to show the impoverishment of our notion of ontology. Laughter, in some way, really *is*; and yet it will not be frozen as subject to some test of existence. It does not so much burst through something as make us suddenly aware of another type of being. Compare the suggestive reading, by Catherine Chalier, of the birth of Isaac. Those who doubt his parentage "remain caught in the perspective...of an ontology which is finite and closed off to any excess" (*restent pris dans l'horizon...d'une ontologie finie et fermée à tout surplus*); Sarah, meanwhile, teaches us "to move forward...in the desire for a surplus of meaning for the world" (*à avancer...dans le désir d'un surplus de sens pour le monde*).[13] That being suddenly aware is crucial: it is another way of saying that laughter is epistemologically significant. An awareness of that other type of being makes us aware of the conceptual straitjackets in which we are enclosed: it is they, perhaps, through which laughter bursts, not being itself.

This extends what we were saying in the previous chapter about language. Our notion of the sayable is also impoverished. We have for the most part a very literal notion of language – what it is, what it does, how it should be organized – in the context of which laughter is simply unintelligible. Partly, laughter is unintelligible because it bespeaks an element of emotion, which is rigidly excluded from rational utterance; partly, because it is not susceptible to analysis in the way in which a statement composed of words – however randomly expressed – may be. This is, as we have seen, because of laughter's radical instability and instantaneity. It cannot be expressed other than from within the instant; it cannot be represented other than within that instant; it cannot be explained.

Instead of rupture, then, can we speak of openness? Laughter expresses an openness to others and otherness: to others apprehended, not as alienated from oneself, but as fleeting extensions of the self – or perhaps, an openness to others and self dissolved. It expresses an openness, more

DOI: 10.1057/9781137370914

generally, to the world, to its uncertainty and instability. Or the dynamic of laughter might be best expressed as an openness to surprise: the surprise of the unknown, the new, the unsayable or the differently sayable. The surprise – thinking of Sarah's laughter – of the impossible.

This openness sets us free from our grounding ontological assumptions. It frees us from assuming that we know what being is. It frees us from the anxious hope that, if we can only represent reality correctly, we shall know what to do next. It frees us from the teleological narrative of our lives – from the sense that, if we put one thing after another we shall eventually come to a successful conclusion. We need not worry about the apparent inevitability of the teleological drive.

Thinking from within the *kairos* of laughter dissolves teleology. The "time for laughter" is a time that can only be experienced on its own terms. It cannot be subsumed into a wider system of the knowable, a structure of sequential or subordinated facts or events. No wonder the fathers of the Christian church were so often at a loss when confronted with Sarah's laughter; it refused absolutely to be subsumed into the teleology of supersessionism or into their notions of eschatology, and could only be subordinated if it were read as something else. No wonder that the more corporeally grounded readings of Sarah's laughter, whether they posit menstruation or try to "hear" the laughter itself, prove more satisfying, while being less submissive to meaning: they remind us of laughter's presence in and only in the moment, of its fluidity, of its uniqueness and yet its susceptibility to the social.

You will notice that this need not be an areligious reading of laughter. I reject the consequential – teleological – sequence of the beatitudes: "Blessed are you that weep now; for you shall laugh ... Woe unto you that laugh now! for you shall mourn and weep" (Luke 6:21 and 25). The point, for me, is not that a certain disposition in this life will automatically have as a result a contrary disposition in heaven. And yet laughter, in its own dissolving disturbing unique moment, in its *kairos*, in its upsetting of all our epistemological presumptions, may be a glimpse of heaven after all. We just know that we shall never know.

# Notes

1   Bergson, "The Idea of Duration," in *Philosophers of Process* ed. D. Browning and W. T. Myers (New York: Fordham University Press, 1998), 140–74.

DOI: 10.1057/9781137370914

2    Zupančič, A. *The Odd One In: On Comedy* (Cambridge, MA: MIT Press, 2008), 146; original emphasis.

3    Parvalescu, A. *Laughter: Notes on a Passion* (Cambridge, MA: MIT Press, 2010), 196, n.2.

4    Nightingale, *Once Out of Nature: Augustine on Time and the Body* (Chicago: University of Chicago Press, 2011), on Augustine's notion of "psychic time," is helpful in thinking about this: see esp. 78–104.

5    For more detailed commentary on these passages, see Conybeare, "Beyond Word and Image: Aural Patterning in Augustine's *Confessions*," in *Envisioning Experience in Late Antiquity and the Middle Ages*, ed. T. F. X. Noble and G. De Nie (Aldershot, England: Ashgate, 2012), and Meijering, E. P. *Augustin über Schöpfung, Ewigkeit und Zeit: Das elfte Buch der Bekenntnisse* (Leiden: Brill, 1979) ad locc.

6    See O'Daly, *Augustine's Philosophy of Mind*, (Berkeley/Los Angeles: University of California Press, 1987) (Berkeley/Los Angeles: University of California Press, 1987) Chapter 6; Pranger, "Time and Narrative in Augustine's *Confessions*," *The Journal of Religion* 81:3 (2001).

7    Stock, *Augustine's Inner Dialogue: The Philosophical Soliloquy in Late Antiquity* (Cambridge: Cambridge University Press, 2010); quotes from 232 and 224 respectively.

8    See also Halliwell on this passage: *Greek Laughter: a Study in Cultural Psychology from Homer to Early Christianity* (Cambridge: Cambridge University Press, 2008), 507–10.

9    Nancy, J-L. *The Birth to Presence* tr. B. Holmes e.a. (Stanford, CA: Stanford University Press, 1993), 5.

10    Many of Nancy's reflections are, however, vitiated once again by a male heterosexual death-driven framework: "it is by laughing that the desire to paint will have penetrated 'into the darkness' of its object, only to discover itself to be the desire to die" (374). No wonder he concludes that what men [*sic*] have in common is the "vulgar" experience of being in the world, "by...the grace of a tart [whore, not pastry!] shaking with laughter" (392).

11    Parvalescu, *Laughter*, 85; in the course of her own discussion of Bataille and *kairos*.

12    The closest approximation in contemporary culture would be the typing of "LOL" in a text message; although how many people actually *are* laughing out loud as they type it? In any case, the approximate and unsatisfactory nature of the substitution of this disembodied shorthand shows by contrast the fullness of the lived experience of laughing.

13    Chalier, C. *Les Matriarches. Sarah, Rébecca, Rachel et Léa* (Paris: Éditions du Cerf, 1985), 59 and 57. The congruence with my reading of laughter seems to me remarkable.

DOI: 10.1057/9781137370914

# Bibliography

## List of works cited

### Ancient and medieval sources

(CCL = Corpus Christianorum Series Latina; CSEL = Corpus Scriptorum Ecclesiasticorum Latinorum; MGH = Monumenta Germaniae Historica; OCT = Oxford Classical Text; PG = Patrologia Graeca; PL = Patrologia Latina; SC = Sources Chrétiennes)

Abelard, *Dialectica* ed. L. M de Rijk, Wijsgerige teksten en studies 1 (Assen: Van Gorcum, 1970²).

Ambrose, *De Abraham* ed. C. Schenkl, CSEL 32, 1 (Vienna 1897).

Ambrose, *De Noe* ed. Schenkl, CSEL 32, 1 (Vienna 1897).

Ambrose, *Epistolae Libri I-VI* ed. O. Faller, CSEL 82, 1 (Vienna 1968).

Ambrose, *Exhortatio Virginitatis*, PL 16, cols. 351–80; ed. Gori, Biblioteca Ambrosiana 14:2 (Milan and Rome, 1989).

Anonymous, *Cena Cypriani* ed. K. Strecker, MGH Poetae Latini Aevi Carolini IV, 2 (Berlin 1923); ed. C. Modesto, *Studien zur* Cena Cypriani *und zu deren Rezeption* (Tübingen 1992).

*Apophthegmata Patrum (collectio alphabetica)*, PG 65, cols. 71–440.

Archpoet, *Die Gedichte des Archipoeta* ed. Wathenphul and Krefeld (Heidelberg: C. Winter, 1958).

Augustine, *De Civitate Dei* ed. B. Dombart and A. Kalb, CCL 47 and 48 (Turnhout 1955).

Augustine, *Confessiones* ed./comm. J. J. O'Donnell, 3 vols. (Oxford: Oxford University Press, 1992; http://www.stoa.org/hippo).

Augustine, *De Doctrina Christiana* ed./tr. R. P. H. Green (Oxford: Oxford University Press, 1995).

Augustine, *Epistulae* ed. Daur, CCL 31, 31A, 31B (Turnhout 2004, 2005, 2009).

Augustine, *De Genesi contra Manichaeos* ed. D. Weber, CSEL 91 (Vienna 1998).

Augustine, *De Libero Arbitrio* ed. W. M. Green, CCL 29 (Turnhout 1970).

Augustine, *De Magistro* ed. K.-D. Daur, CCL 29 (Turnhout 1970).

Augustine, *Quaestiones super Genesim* ed. I. Fraipont, CCL 33 (Turnhout 1958).

Basil of Caesarea, *Regulae Brevius Tractatae*, PG 31 cols. 1051–1506.

Basil of Caesarea, *Regulae Fusius Tractatae*, PG 31 cols. 889–1052.

Cicero, *De Re Publica: Selections* ed. J. Zetzel (Cambridge, UK: Cambridge University Press, 1995).

Clement of Alexandria, *Paedagogus I-III* ed. H.-I. Marrou, SC 70, 108, 158 (Paris 1960, 1965, 1970).

Clement of Alexandria, *Stromata*, PG 8 cols. 685–1382; multiple volumes of SC.

*Genesis*, tr. and comm. R. Alter (New York and London: Norton, 1996).

Gregory of Nazianzus, *Poemata historica: Epitaphia*, PG 38 cols. 11–82.

Jerome, *Commentarius in Ecclesiasten* ed. Adriaen, CCL 72 (Turnhout 1959).

Jerome, *Hebraicae Quaestiones in libro Geneseos*, ed. de Lagarde, CCL 72 (Turnhout 1959).

John Chrysostom, *Homiliae in Genesim,* PG 53 and 54.

John Chrysostom, *Homiliae in Epistulam ad Hebraeos*, PG 63 cols. 9–236.

*Midrash Rabbah: Genesis* tr. H. Freedman, 2 vols. (Oxford 1939).

Origen, *Homiliae in Genesim* tr. Rufinus, ed. Doutreleau, intr. De Lubac and Doutreleau, SC 72 (Paris 1976).

Philo, *De Abrahamo* ed. Gorez, Les Oeuvres de Philon d'Alexandrie 20–21 (Paris 1966).

Philo, *De Mutatione Nominum* ed. Arnaldez, Les Oeuvres de Philon d'Alexandrie 18 (Paris 1964).

Philo, *De Praemiis et Poenis* ed. Beckaert, Les Oeuvres de Philon d'Alexandrie 27 (Paris 1961).

DOI: 10.1057/9781137370914

Philo, *De Sacrificiis Abelis et Caini*, ed. Méasson, Les Oeuvres de Philon d'Alexandrie 4 (Paris 1966).

Plato, *Theaetetus* ed. Burnet, OCT; tr. and ann., J. McDowell (Oxford: Clarendon Press, 1973).

Plotinus, *Enneads* IV tr. A. H. Armstrong, Loeb Classical Library (Cambridge, MA: Harvard University Press, 1984).

Porphyry, *On the Life of Plotinus* tr. A. H. Armstrong, Loeb Classical Library (Cambridge, MA: Harvard University Press, 1966).

*The Qur'an* tr. M. A. S. Abdel Haleem (Oxford: Oxford University Press, 2004).

Rashi, *Commentary on Bereishis/Genesis* tr. and ann., elucidated by Y. Herczeg (Brooklyn NY: Mesorah Publications, 1995).

Al-Ṭabarī, Abū Jaʿfar Muḥammad b. Jarīr, *Jamiʿ al-Bayān ʿan taʾwīl al-Qurʾān* ed. Ṣalāḥ ʿAbdal-Fattāḥ al-Khālidī (Damascus: Dār al-Qalam, 1997). Cited in text simply as "Tabari".

Al-Ṭabarī, *The History of al-Ṭabarī*, volume II: *Prophets and Patriarchs*, tr. W. Brinner (Albany: State University of New York Press, 1987).

Zeno of Verona, *Tractatus* ed. B. Löfstedt, CCL 22 (Turnhout 1971).

## Modern sources

Abécassis, A. "Le rire des patriarches", *Lumière et vie* 230 (December 1996), 7–14.

Adolf, H. "On Mediaeval Laughter", *Speculum* 22 (1947), 251–3.

Agamben, G. *Potentialities* (Stanford CA: Stanford University Press, 2000).

Ammann, L. *Vorbild und Vernunft: Die Regelung von Lachen und Scherzen im mittelalterlichen Islam* (Hildesheim/Zürich/New York: G. Olms, 1993).

Arendt, H. *The Human Condition* intr. M. Canovan (Chicago: University of Chicago Press, 1998; first published 1958).

Auerbach, E. *Mimesis: The Representation of Reality in Western Literature* tr. W. Trask (1953), new intro. E. Said (Princeton, NJ: Princeton University Press, 2003; first published in German, 1946).

Baconsky, T. *Le rire des Pères. Essai sur le rire dans la patristique grecque* (Paris: Desclée de Brouwer, 1996).

Bakhtin, M. *Rabelais and His World* tr. H. Iswolsky (Cambridge, MA: MIT Press, 1968; first published in Russian, 1965).

Bal, M. (ed.) "Anti-convenant. Counter-reading women's lives in the Hebrew Bible", *Journal for the Study of the Old Testament* Supplement Series 81 (Sheffield, England: Almond Press, 1989).

DOI: 10.1057/9781137370914

Barthes, R. *Le plaisir du texte* (Paris: Éditions du Seuil, 1973); *The Pleasure of the Text* tr. R. Miller (New York: Farrar, Straus and Giroux, 1975).

Barton, C. "Savage miracles: the redemption of lost honor in Roman society and the sacrament of the gladiator and the martyr", *Representations* 45 (1994), 41–71.

Baskin, J. R. *Midrashic Women: Formations of the Feminine in Rabbinic Literature* (Hanover, NH, and London: Brandeis University Press, 2002).

Baudelaire, C. "De l'essence du rire, et généralement du comique dans les arts plastiques", in Baudelaire, *Oeuvres complètes* ed. C. Pichois (Paris: Gallimard, 1975), 2: 525–43.

Beauvoir, S. de, *The Ethics of Ambiguity* tr. B. Frechtman (New York: Philosophical Library, 1948).

Bergson, H. *Le Rire: essai sur la signification du comique* (Paris: Quadrige/ PUF, 1940; first published 1900); English translation by W. Sypher in *Comedy* (Baltimore and London: Johns Hopkins University Press, 1956), 61–190.

Bergson, H. "The Idea of Duration", in *Philosophers of Process* ed. D. Browning and W. T. Myers (New York: Fordham University Press, 1998), 140–74.

Bersani, L. "Sociality and Sexuality", *Critical Inquiry* 26 (2000), 641–56.

Betz, H. D. *The Greek Magical Papyri in Translation* vol. 1 (Chicago: Chicago University Press, 1992).

Biddick, K. *The Typological Imaginary: Circumcision, Typology, History* (Philadelphia: University of Pennsylvania Press, 2003).

Braet, H., G. Latré, and W. Verbeke, *Risus Mediaevalis: Laughter in Medieval Literature and Art* (Leuven: Leuven University Press, 2003).

Bremmer, J. and H. Roodenberg (ed.) *A Cultural History of Humour from Antiquity to the Present Day* (Cambridge, UK: Polity Press, 1997).

Brenner, A. "On the semantic field of humour, laughter and the comic in the Old Testament", in *On Humour and the Comic in the Hebrew Bible*, Bible and Literature Series 23 ed. Radday and Brenner (Sheffield: Almond Press, 1990), 39–58.

Butler, J. *Undoing Gender* (New York and London: Routledge, 2004).

Cavarero, A. "The Maidservant from Thrace", in eadem, *In Spite of Plato: A Feminist Rewriting of Ancient Philosophy* (New York and London: Routledge, 1995).

Cavarero, A. *For More than One Voice. Towards a Philosophy of Vocal Expression* tr. P. A. Kottman (Stanford CA: Stanford University Press, 2005; first published in Italian, 2003).

DOI: 10.1057/9781137370914

Chalier, C. *Les Matriarches. Sarah, Rébecca, Rachel et Léa* (Paris: Éditions du Cerf, 1985).

Cixous, H. "The Laugh of the Medusa", *Signs* (Summer 1976), 875–93; revised version of 'Le rire de la méduse', *L'arc* (1975), 39–54.

Colish, M. *Ambrose's Patriarchs: Ethics for the Common Man* (Notre Dame, IN: University of Notre Dame Press, 2005).

Conybeare, C. *Paulinus Noster: Self and Symbols in the Letters of Paulinus of Nola* (Oxford: Oxford University Press, 2000).

Conybeare, C. "The Ambiguous Laughter of Saint Laurence", *Journal of Early Christian Studies* 10 (2002), 175–202.

Conybeare, C. *The Irrational Augustine* (Oxford: Oxford University Press, 2006).

Conybeare, C. "*sanctum, lector, percense uolumen*: Snakes, Readers, and the Whole Text in Prudentius' *Hamartigenia*", in *The Early Christian Book* ed. W. Klingshirn and L. Safran (Washington DC: Catholic University of America Press, 2007), 225–40.

Conybeare, C. "Beyond Word and Image: Aural Patterning in Augustine's *Confessions*", in *Envisioning Experience in Late Antiquity and the Middle Ages* ed. T. F. X. Noble and G. De Nie (Aldershot, England: Ashgate, 2012).

Curtius, E. R. *European Literature and the Latin Middle Ages* tr. W. Trask (London: Routledge and Kegan Paul, 1953; new ed. with afterword by P. Godman, Princeton: Princeton University Press, 1990; first published in German, 1948).

Critchley, S. *On Humour* (London/New York: Routledge, 2002).

Critchley, S. *Infinitely Demanding: Ethics of Commitment, Politics of Resistance* (London/New York: Verso, 2007).

Darwin, C. "A Biographical Sketch of an Infant", *Mind* 2 (1877), 285–94.

Derrida, J. *Writing and Difference* tr. A. Bass (Chicago: University of Chicago Press, 1978; first published in French, 1967).

DuBois, Page *Sappho is Burning* (Chicago: University of Chicago Press, 1995).

Eco, U. *The Name of the Rose* tr. William Weaver (London: Secker & Warburg, 1983).

Ellison, R. "An Extravagance of Laughter", in *Going to the Territory* (New York: Random House, 1986).

Emerson, C. "Coming to Terms with Bakhtin's Carnival: Ancient, Modern, sub Specie Aeternitatis", in *Bakhtin and the Classics* ed. R. Bracht Branham (Evanston, IL: Northwestern University Press, 2002), 5–26.

DOI: 10.1057/9781137370914

Freud, S. *The Joke and its Relation to the Unconscious* tr. J. Crick, intr. J. Cary (London: Penguin, 2003; first published in German, Leipzig/Vienna 1905).

Freud, S. "Humour", in *Collected Papers* vol. 5, ed. James Strachey (London/New York: The Psycho-Analytical Press, 1950).

Gilhus, Ingvild Sælid, *Laughing Gods, Weeping Virgins: Laughter in the History of Religion* (London/New York: Routledge, 1997).

Glei, R. F. "Ridebat de facto Sarra. Bemerkungen zur *Cena Cypriani*", in *Literaturparodie in Antike und Mittelalter* ed. W. Ax and R. F. Glei, 153–70 (Trier: Bochumer Altertumswissenschaftliches Colloquium 15, 1993).

Glenn, P. *Laughter in Interaction*, Studies in Interactional Sociolinguistics (Cambridge: Cambridge University Press, 2003).

Goldstein, D. M. *Laughter Out of Place: Race, Class, Violence, and Sexuality in a Rio Shantytown* (Berkeley/Los Angeles/London: University of California Press, 2003).

Gourévitch, A. "Le comique et le sérieux dans la littérature religieuse du moyen age", *Diogène* 90 (1975), 67–89.

Grosz, E. *Jacques Lacan: A Feminist Introduction* (London/New York: Routledge, 1990).

Halliwell, S. *Greek Laughter: A Study in Cultural Psychology from Homer to Early Christianity* (Cambridge: Cambridge University Press, 2008).

Halsall, G. (ed.) *Humour, History and Politics in Late Antiquity and the Early Middle Ages* (Cambridge: Cambridge University Press, 2002).

Havrelock, R. "The Myth of Birthing the Hero: Heroic Barrenness in the Hebrew Bible", *Biblical Interpretation* 16 (2008), 154–78.

Higgins, K. M. "Waves of Uncountable Laughter", in *Nietzsche's Futures* ed. J. Lippitt (Basingstoke: Macmillan, 1999), 82–98.

Hobbes, T. *Human Nature*, in *The English Works of Thomas Hobbes* ed. W. Molesworth, vol. 4 (London: John Bohn, 1840; first published 1640), 1–76.

Holtzman, L. " 'Does God Really Laugh?' – Appropriate and Inappropriate Descriptions of God in Islamic Traditionalist Theology", in *Laughter in the Middle Ages and Early Modern Times: Epistemology of a Fundamental Human Behavior, its Meaning, and Consequences* ed. A. Classen (Berlin/New York: De Gruyter, 2010), 165–200.

Huizinga, J. *Homo Ludens: A Study of the Play Element in Culture* (Boston: Beacon Press, 1950; first published in German, 1944).

DOI: 10.1057/9781137370914

Irigaray, L. "Sorcerer Love: A Reading of Plato, *Symposium*, 'Diotima's Speech'", in *An Ethics of Sexual Difference* tr. C. Burke and G. Gill (London: Athlone Press, 1993; first published in French, 1984), 20–33.

Irigaray, L. *The Way of Love* (London and New York: Continuum, 2002).

Isaak, J. *Feminism and Contemporary Art. The Revolutionary Power of Women's Laughter* (London: Routledge, 1996).

Jantzen, G. *Becoming Divine* (Manchester: Manchester University Press, 1998).

Jantzen, G. "'Promising Ashes': A Queer Language of Life", in *Queer Theology: Rethinking the Western Body* ed. G. Loughlin (Oxford: Blackwell, 2007), 245–53.

Joubert, L. *Treatise on Laughter* tr. De Rocher (Tuscaloosa, AL: University of Alabama Press, 1980; first published in French, 1579).

Katz, C. E. *Levinas, Judaism, and the Feminine: The Silent Footsteps of Rebecca* (Bloomington, IN: Indiana University Press, 2003).

Kierkegaard, S. *Fear and Trembling* tr. H. and E. Hong, Kierkegaard's Writings VI (Princeton, NJ: Princeton University Press, 1983; first published in Swedish, 1843).

Koestler, A. *The Act of Creation* (New York: Macmillan, 1964).

Kofman, S. *Pourquoi rit-on? Freud et le mot d'esprit* (Paris: Éditions galilée, 1986).

Kristeva, J. "Stabat Mater", in eadem, *Histoires d'amour* (Paris: Éditions Denoël, 1983), 225–47.

Kristeva, J. *Revolution in Poetic Language* (New York: Columbia University Press, 1984; first published in French, 1974.)

Kristeva, J. "The Semiotic and the Symbolic", in *The Women and Language Debate: A Sourcebook* ed. C. Roman, S. Juhasz, and C. Miller (New Brunswick, NJ: Rutgers University Press,1994), 45–55.

Krueger, D. "The Old Testament in Monasticism", in *The Old Testament in Byzantium*, ed. Paul Magdalino and Robert Nelson (Washington DC: Dumbarton Oaks, 2010), 199–221.

Lacan, J. *Feminine Sexuality: Jacques Lacan and the école Freudienne*, ed. J. Mitchell and J. Rose, tr. J. Rose (New York: W. W. Norton and Company, 1982).

Lachmann, R. "Bakhtin and Carnival: Culture as Counter-Culture", *Cultural Critique* 11 (Winter, 1988–9), 115–52.

Le Goff, J. "Le rire dans les règles monastiques du haut Moyen Âge", in idem, *Haut Moyen Âge: Culture, Éducation et Société* (La Garenne-Colombes 1990), 93–103.

DOI: 10.1057/9781137370914

Lerer, S. *Children's Literature: A Reader's History, from Aesop to Harry Potter* (Chicago and London: University of Chicago Press, 2008).

Lippitt, J. "Nietzsche, Zarathustra and the Status of Laughter", *British Journal of Aesthetics* 32 (1992), 39–49.

Lippitt, J. "Humour and Incongruity", *Cogito* 8 (1994), 147–53.

Lippitt, J. "Humour and Superiority", *Cogito* 9 (1995), 54–61.

Lippitt, J. "Humour and Release", *Cogito* 9 (1995), 169–76.

Lippitt, J. "Existential Laughter", *Cogito* 10 (1996), 63–72.

Lloyd Morgan, C. "Laughter", in *Encyclopaedia of Religion and Ethics* vol. VII (New York/Edinburgh: Charles Scribner's Sons, 1915).

Mathewes, C. "The Liberation of Questioning in Augustine's *Confessions*", *Journal of the American Academy of Religion* 30 (2002), 539–60.

Mazzucco, C. (ed.) *Riso e comicità nel cristianesimo antico* (Alessandria: Edizioni dell'orso, 2007).

Meijering, E. P. *Augustin über Schöpfung, Ewigkeit und Zeit: Das elfte Buch der Bekenntnisse* (Leiden: Brill, 1979).

Minois, G. *Histoire du rire et de la dérision* (Paris: Fayard, 2000).

Modesto, C. *Studien zur* Cena Cypriani *und zu deren Rezeption*, Classica Monacensia 3 (Tübingen: Gunter Narr Verlag, 1992).

Morreall, J. *Taking Laughter Seriously* (Albany NY: State University of New York Press, 1983).

Morrison, T. *Song of Solomon* (New York: Random House, 1977).

Moore, F. C. T. *Bergson: Thinking Backwards* (Cambridge: Cambridge University Press, 1996).

Mosetti Casaretto, F. (ed.) *Il Riso. Capacità di ridere e pratica del riso nelle civiltà medievali*, Atti delle I Giornate Internazionali Interdisciplinari di Studio sul Medioevo, Siena, 2–4 Ottobre 2002 (Alessandria: Edizioni dell'orso, 2005).

Mosetti Casaretto, F. "Modelli e antimodelli per la 'Cena Cypriani': il 'teatro interiore', Zenone e... Apuleio!" *Wiener Studien* 119 (2006), 215–46.

Nancy, J-L. *The Birth to Presence* tr. B. Holmes et al. (Stanford, CA: Stanford University Press, 1993).

Nightingale, A. *Once Out of Nature: Augustine on Time and the Body* (Chicago: University of Chicago Press, 2011).

O'Daly, G. *Augustine's Philosophy of Mind* (Berkeley/Los Angeles: University of California Press, 1987).

Opie, I. and Opie, P. *The Lore and Language of Schoolchildren* (Oxford: Oxford University Press, 1959).

DOI: 10.1057/9781137370914

Orme, N. "Children and Literature in Medieval England", *Medium Aevum* 68 (1999), 218–46.

Parvalescu, A. *Laughter: Notes on a Passion* (Cambridge, MA: MIT Press, 2010).

Pin-Fat, V. *Universality, Ethics and International Relations: A Grammatical Reading* (London and New York: Routledge, 2010).

Plessner, H. *Laughing and Crying: A Study of the Limits of Human Behavior* tr. Spencer Churchill and Grene (Evanston, IL: Northwestern University Press, 1970; first published in German as *Lachen und Weinen*, 1961).

Pranger, M. B. "Time and Narrative in Augustine's *Confessions*", *The Journal of Religion* 81:3 (2001), 377–93.

Provine, R. R. "Laughter", *American Scientist* 84:1 (1996).

Provine, R. R. *Laughter: A Scientific Investigation* (New York: Viking, 2000).

Prusak, B. "Le rire à Nouveau: Rereading Bergson", in *Journal of Aesthetics and Art Criticism* 62 (2004), 377–88.

Prusak, B. "The Science of Laughter: Helmuth Plessner's *Laughing and Crying* Revisited", *Continental Philosophy Review* 38 (2006), 41–69.

Rabelais, F. *Gargantua* intr./ann. G. Defaux (Paris: Librairie Générale Française, 1994; first published 1535).

Radday, Y. T. and Brenner, A. (ed.) *On Humour and the Comic in the Hebrew Bible* Bible and Literature Series 23 (Sheffield: Almond Press, 1990).

Röcke, W. and H. R. Velten (ed.) *Lachgemeinschaften. Kulturelle Inszenierungen und soziale Wirkungen von Gelächter im Mittelalter und in der Frühen Neuzeit* Trends in Medieval Philology 4 (Berlin/New York: De Gruyter, 2005).

Rosenwein, B. *Emotional Communities in the Early Middle Ages* (Ithaca and London: Cornell University Press, 2006).

Sarrazin, B. "Jésus n'a jamais ri. Histoire d'un lieu commun", *Recherches de science religieuse* 82 (1994), 217–22.

Skinner, Q. "Hobbes and the Classical Theory of Laughter", in idem, *Visions of Politics* vol. 3 (Cambridge: Cambridge University Press, 2002), 142–76.

Smolak, K. " 'De circumstantibus ridere nonnulli'. Aspekte des Lachens in der Kultur der Spätantike", in Mosetti Casaretto (ed.), *Il Riso*, 31–48.

Snediker, M. *Queer Optimism: Lyric Personhood and Other Felicitous Persuasions* (Minneapolis, MN: University of Minnesota Press, 2008).

DOI: 10.1057/9781137370914

Sroufe, L. A. and E. Waters, "The Ontogenesis of Smiling and Laughter: A Perspective on the Organization of Development in Infancy", *Psychological Review* 83 (1976), 173–89.

Sternstein, M. "Laughter, Gesture, and Flesh: Kafka's 'In the Penal Colony'", *Modernism/Modernity* 8 (2001), 315–23.

Stock, B. *The Implications of Literacy: Written Language and Models of Interpretation in the Eleventh and Twelfth Centuries* (Princeton: Princeton University Press, 1983).

Stock, B. *Listening for the Text: On the Uses of the Past* (Philadelphia: University of Pennsylvania Press, 1990).

Stock, B. *Augustine's Inner Dialogue: The Philosophical Soliloquy in Late Antiquity* (Cambridge: Cambridge University Press, 2010).

Stowasser, B. *Women in the Qur'an, Traditions, and Interpretation* (New York: Oxford University Press, 1994).

Stroumsa, G. G. "Christ's Laughter: Docetic Origins Reconsidered", *Journal of Early Christian Studies* 12 (2004), 267–88.

Sully, J. *An Essay on Laughter: Its Forms, Its Causes, Its Development and Its Value* (London, New York, Bombay: Longmans, Green, and co., 1902).

Tamer, G. "The Qur'an and Humor", in Tamer (ed.), *Humor in der arabischen Kultur* (Berlin: De Gruyter, 2009), 3–28.

Tatlock, J. S. P. "Mediaeval Laughter", *Speculum* 21 (1946), 289–94.

Zornberg, A. G. *The Beginning of Desire: Reflections on Genesis* (New York: Image/Doubleday, 1995).

Zupančič, A. *The Odd One In: On Comedy* (Cambridge, MA: MIT Press, 2008).

DOI: 10.1057/9781137370914

# Index

*Note:* The terms "Sarah", "Abraham", and "laughter" are so ubiquitous that I have not indexed them separately.

DOI: 10.1057/9781137370914

DOI: 10.1057/9781137370914

CPSIA information can be obtained at www.ICGtesting.com
Printed in the USA
LVOW11*0356141014

408543LV00004BA/18/P